Centerpieces Made Easy

To my husband Gregg...
Without his unwavering support, love, and belief in me, I would not have dreamed of writing a book.
We are the perfect partners in business, but mostly in life.

To my wife Sandi...
I would have never done this without your experience, support and love. You're my best friend and love,
and make this all a great ride!

We wish to acknowledge John Obad, Venue Owner of Courtyard D'ORO, Old Sacramento, CA., Business Associate, for allowing us to use his venue and pictures shown on
Pages 40, 41, 61, 63, 65, & 91.

All photography completed by and property of Sandi's Design except for:
Page 59 and back cover (R) by Stout Photo - Jessica Stout
Pages 10 top (R), 40, 41 & 91 by Alba Fiore - Dawn Spinella,
Pages 67 & 74 by Modern Grace Images - Shawna Clark
Pages 38 & 66 by Linda Boyko, Business Associate.
We want to thank them for the use of their beautiful pictures.
Centerpieces Made Easy Copyright © 2013 by Sandi and Gregg Allcut

All rights reserved. Printed in the United States of America. No part of this publication shall be reproduced, transmitted or resold in whole or in part in any form, without the prior written consent of the authors. All trademarks and registered trademarks appearing in Centerpieces Made Easy are the property of their respective owners.

The information contained in Centerpieces Made Easy is meant to serve as a comprehensive collection of time-tested and proven centerpiece strategies that the authors of the Book have sold and used in actual weddings. Recommendations by the authors and reading this book does not guarantee or warrantee that one's results will exactly mirror our own results. The authors of Centerpieces Made Easy have made all reasonable efforts to provide current and accurate information for the readers of this Book. The authors will not be held liable for any unintentional errors or omissions that may be found.

The purpose of this book is to educate and entertain. The material in Centerpieces Made Easy may include information, products, or services by third parties. Third Party materials comprise of the products and opinions expressed by their owners. As such, the authors of this guide do not assume responsibility or liability for any Third Party Material or opinions.

The publication of such Third Party materials does not constitute the authors' guarantee of any information, instruction, opinion, products or service contained within the Third Party Material. Use of recommended Third Party Material does not guarantee that your results will mirror our own.

The book identifies product names and services known to be trademarks, registered trademarks, or service marks of their respective holders. They are the property of their respective owners and are used throughout this book in an editorial fashion only. The authors are not associated with any product or vendor mentioned in this book.

The author and publisher shall not be held liable or responsible to any person and/or entity for any loss or damage caused, or alleged to have been caused, directly or indirectly by the information contained in this book.

Whether because of the general evolution of the Internet, or the unforeseen changes in company policy and editorial submission guidelines, what is stated as fact at the time of this writing, may become outdated or simply inapplicable at a later date.

This may apply to the supplier's websites platform, as well as, the various similar companies that we have referenced in this Book. Great effort has been exerted to safeguard the accuracy of this writing.

ISBN-13: 978-0615809908 (Centerpieces Made Easy)

ISBN-10: 0615809901

Inside

Introduction	1
Determining Your Look... Just Imagine!	2
How Will Your Guest Tables Look?	6
The Use of Color	8
So How Much Will You Save?	11
Tips and Preparation	12
Enhancements... So Many Choices	23
Making Perfect Bows Everytime	28
Simple and Elegant... From Start to Finish!!!	30
Simple to do... Easy on the Budget	36
A Citrus Fruit Arrangement... Summer Time	40
Flowers with... Citrus Slices	42
When a Bud Vase... Is Not Just a Bud Vase	45
Floating Flowers... So Easy	51
Floating Flowers... Making it Crystal Clear	53
Floating Candles... Vases, Votives & Blooms	55
Tall, Dramatic and Easy... Standing Tall	59
Tall, Dramatic and Easy... Designed with Flair	61
Rings of Beauty... Simply Done	66
Rings of Beauty... Done Well	69
Start with the Basics... Make it Your Own!	76
Flowers With Double Duty... Dual Use	84
Hydrangea... Effortless Elegance	86
Small and Simple... A Perfect Touch	88
Head Table	90
Napkin Décor	92
Appendix A... Centerpiece Cost Worksheet	94
Appendix B... Tools and Supplies	95
Appendix C... Table Diagrams	96
Appendix D... List of Suppliers	103

Introduction

You are in the spotlight of a very special event... you are the decision maker of your wedding, reception, or a very special occasion. With so much to plan, organize and prepare, deciding the colors, theme and décor are just a few of the most important decisions you will make. You are setting the ambiance of your event. Bringing everything together from color to candles, linens to lighting, floral design to décor, all are very important to the success of your very special event.

Planning a wedding or event can be overwhelming and the first thought and question is usually "where should I begin?" Then a little stress may set in, or maybe a lot of stress... maybe your budget is not as much as you wish and you wonder if everything you envision will fit into your budget. So getting some ideas, planning tips and budget friendly help is vital. It is not only vital, it saves time, money and your energy. **Tips will help stretch your budget.**

One of the items in the budget would be the cost of flowers. Flowers can be expensive, but they are what make an event come to life. Flowers offer color, style, and they can reflect you. What is a wedding picture without the beauty of flowers? So the next question is how to have the flowers you want and save money at the same time.

By doing your own centerpieces you will save the cost of what the florist would charge to do them. It is work, but with dependable help and the right design, you can save several hundred dollars in your centerpieces alone. Being organized, planning ahead and being prepared will result in having a centerpiece that will cost less, and have more value.

There are many books available with DIY centerpieces with unrealistic expectations and would cost more than the budget you may have for flowers. The difference in our book is that you can actually do these centerpieces! We have illustrated them with step by step instructions including over 450 pictures. We also keep the budget in mind. We have ideas from the very simple bud vase, to the more elaborate set-up that you can enhance as much as you like.

Now... what you need is a basic menu of centerpiece design ideas that are easy to do and will show you step-by-step how to design them from start to finish. There are centerpiece ideas in our book that truly ***ANYONE can create***. We have purposely selected centerpiece ideas that are simple to do even if you have no floral experience, and that can be delegated to dependable helpers. You can choose a centerpiece with as many flowers as you wish, or a centerpiece using silks, candles, no candles, add or change as much or as little to the design as you wish by varying the centerpieces to reflect you... It is all up to you. **A beautiful centerpiece is in your budget!**

If you do not have floral experience, that shouldn't be the reason you decide not to do your own centerpieces. With the step-by-step instructions and pictures, anyone can be the designer of their own centerpieces. We give you lots of tips, planning suggestions and examples of basic designs and set-ups of the design. Chose a design and with practice, it becomes a beautiful centerpiece for your wedding.

Add your dependable helpers of family and friends... and you can do it!

Determining Your Look.... Just Imagine!

Determining the look of your Décor and Flowers for your wedding will be based on some decisions you've made or will be making. A few of those decisions involve:

The Venue	Your Colors
Time of Year	Time of Day
Choosing a Theme	Your Favorite Flowers
Style of Dresses	Time Dedication for Flowers

The Venue - What are the colors used by the venue in their decor, what is the ceiling height, is it indoors or outdoors, or what is the size of the reception room? ...Backup plan for rain?

Your Colors - The colors you have chosen for your wedding... does it blend with the colors of the venue? Or do you need to incorporate some of their color, and how are you going to blend color, flowers, linens and décor with your ideas? What is your plan to make your wedding reflect YOU?!

~ 2 ~   Centerpieces Made Easy

The *Time of Year* and the *Time of Day* are critical to your planning.
Your flowers will be like the icing on the cake. Making sure your favorite flowers are available and in-season for the wedding is an important question to ask your floral vendor. If you are having a summer outdoor wedding, where 90 degree weather, or even warmer is a possibility, then the choice of flowers and how they are prepared is crucial for success. Wilted flowers are not pretty in wedding pictures!

Choosing a Theme - Many couples choose a theme, some simple, some elaborate. For example, we had a bride that named the tables after cars instead of giving them a table number. As a surprise for the groom, she made the groom's cake a race car. Hobbies and special interests make a great theme. We have had themes of boats, songs and even rock group names. In this chapter we have an example of a golf theme for a groom that loved golf. An elaborate theme could be a Roaring 20's party with guests dressing in the appropriate attire. Whatever you chose, planning the details make a difference in the look of your wedding.

Choosing a Centerpiece - Choosing to do your centerpieces will take organization, planning and lots of dependable help. Our book with over 450 pictures has step by step instructions, tips for your success, and set up of the design. We have also included ideas on how to enhance your centerpieces once you've completed them. Our book is truly for the person who wants to save money, be creative without any floral design experience, and put the personal touch in their wedding.

But it does take some work and planning.

Some of the centerpieces can be prepared months ahead of time. Some will take several days to prepare right before the wedding.
Know your limits.

If you are a part of the wedding... such as the bride, bridesmaid or the mother of the bride, you need to look beautiful for the pictures. So... a plan is needed to get everything prepared, transported, and set up. Choosing the people who help need to be dependable, they will be the ones to carry out your plan on the day of your event.

Practicing is the best way to determine the amount of time needed to design your flowers, determine the cost, and which centerpiece you like the best. Try more than one!

Pick a theme and be creative. It does take some planning and preparation, but you will hit a hole in one with your guests. At the end of the night your centerpieces can be gifts for people who have been especially helpful or they can be raffled off for extra fun.

A theme can make an event so much fun. An idea for a theme can come from a hobby, career, sports or just something you really love. Pick the theme and start planning.

Each centerpiece can be different, or all the same. If you have 15 tables, create three centerpiece designs, and then plan to make five of each centerpiece. Consistency with the flowers and theme will bring it all together.

This is so much fun to do and create!

This event was a fun one! The groom was a golfer and so the theme was a natural choice. We started Adventure Shopping for all the fun things for our décor. We found golf clubs, books, golf themed mugs, and bud vases. We borrowed the golfer's shoes, golf towels, golf balls and golf tees.

The photo above with the book on *Passion* has a bud vase placed in between the pages. To make the bud vase see our chapter, *When a Bud Vase... Is Not Just a Bud Vase.*

The flowers in the golf themed mug could be arranged one of two ways. See our chapter on *Small and Simple... A Perfect Touch*, or our chapter on *Start with the Basics... Make It Your Own!* The arrangement is no bigger than 5-6 inches in diameter.

We added a mini-putting green as a companion piece. Use a small piece of floral foam in a container like a small plastic plant liner (3 inches in diameter and one inch in height, plant liners you can cut to the height you want).

Cover the floral foam with some greenery or moss. For a realistic look, use a ground cover grass or artificial-turf which is both available at a home improvement store. Stick a golf tee through the "putting green". Glue a golf ball on top of the tee.

The golf shoe arrangement was a favorite! Make the flower arrangement in a small plant liner, the size of the shoe opening. Using the instructions from our chapter, *Start with the Basics... Make It Your Own!* you can design the flowers for the shoes. You will make a smaller basic design to fit your shoe. Set the shoes up on golf towels and you have your centerpiece done.

Our golf club centerpiece was fun to do. To attach the golf club to a decorative wood base we drilled a hole up through the bottom, and screwed the golf club in place and... now... ready to take a swing!

Set a piece of floral foam on the base and cover with greenery or moss. Arrange the flowers as desired. If you want to make it even simpler, use small potted plants. Small four inch plants in clay pots work great.

The picture showing the arrangement against the wall was the buffet piece. If you look closely, there is a bridge outlined with little battery operated lights. At the end, a putting green complete with the flag identifying the hole. The flowers were tall stemmed flowers and greens arranged in floral foam. Make it look like outdoors and a part of nature.

We chose different types of greenery and Myrtle for height. Our main flowers were Alstroemeria, Spray Roses, and wild-type flowers. Any type flowers would be good for these designs.

These centerpieces can all have a different design and be made with fresh or silk flowers. Making your centerpieces out of silk flowers allows most of the preparation to be done well before the event.

Then the only thing left to do is... Have fun!

How Will Your Guests Tables Look?

Your reception area may not be this large, but the planning, coordination and all the details are important no matter the size of the event. The centerpieces are all the basic centerpieces that are in our book but they are expanded and are on a much larger scale. The roses in the picture are 5 feet tall and are arranged in a trumpet vase 28 inches in height... essentially, it is just an exceptionally large bud vase.

The centerpiece in the foreground that is sitting on top of a vase filled with pomegranates (grown by the groom), and the centerpieces with the fiber optic lights are both basic arrangements (*Start With The Basics... Make It Your Own!*) that you can make with our step-by-step design instructions. We wouldn't suggest starting out with some of these centerpieces, but with some practice... you never know what you can do!

The first part of your plan is to think in detail, write out a plan, and practice. It is a must to think of the bigger picture. Planning the ceremony flowers for a dual use helps decorate the reception. After the ceremony, have a diagram of where the décor will be placed at the reception. Your helpers will know exactly what they will be moving and where. With a plan, and good help, the look of your room will be beautiful.

All these reception rooms have something in common. Planning and preparation in all the details of the wedding was the key to their event going smoothly. A reliable helper carried out the set up the bride envisioned. The helper was involved in the planning process and when the day came, they knew exactly what to do without having to run and ask the bride. Delegate, enjoy the day, without stressing over the set up!

The Use of Color

Color is important! Color and flowers are what bring your guest tables and reception room alive. How will your guests view your room as they walk in? Will it be welcoming and provide lots of interest? Will the room have a warm glow (if your event is in cool weather), or will it look like it could use more planning.

If you have decided on your colors, or still need to decide, it might be helpful to go to your local home improvement store and get some paint color samples. Color will differ, may not exactly match and colors can't be carried in your memory. It is amazing how far off the color can be when buying something you think is your color. By carrying some samples of your color, you will save time and money. Time, by not having to return something, and money wasted because it didn't end up working they way you thought. The color(s) of your girl's dresses are fashion colors that may or may not be a color readily available in the stores when looking for décor items… and flowers definitely don't come in all the fashion colors. ***The idea is to blend, contrast and compliment***. Colors can be beautiful and not match. Experiment with color!

An example for adding color on the guest's tables would be to give some thought about the use of color when renting your linens. **Make the linen rental work for you.** When deciding on your linen color, your table cloth could be a different color than your napkins. Depending on the room, white linens can be a lot of blank space. An example of color use in a coral and yellow wedding would be a coral table cloth and a yellow napkin, yellow vase, with yellows, coral or a white flower. Or you could reverse the colors, yellow linen, peach or coral napkin, and a coral or peach vase with a yellow rose or white flower, yellow or coral ribbon. You could even make it half and half of each color scheme! We have included pictures of this color scheme in this chapter.

Adding color to the décor of the guest's tables provides interest and it personalizes your event.
Popular enhancement choices are: mirrors, petals, metallic confetti (check with the venue before using), colored submersible LED lights for the warmer weather, and candles for the cooler temperatures (candles can have so many looks), flower blooms, mini replicas of hobbies or special interests. Enhancements with the centerpiece can be unique as personal pictures in colored frames of the bride and groom as children, or a variety of engagement pictures. So many ideas to add color! Go with what you love!

Wedding favors done in your wedding colors sitting at your guest's place setting adds a personal touch and décor at the same time. Ideas of the wedding favors are endless. We have had a chef make a bottled special sauce with a bride and groom label, CD's featuring the bride and groom's favorite songs with the cover in wedding colors, little jars of jelly made by the bride's mother, mason jars filled with Jelly Belly Jelly Beans in their wedding colors tied with a special thank you… think of something that reflects you!

For guest seating, identify their table with a theme or a personal interest. Make personalized stand-up table cards to set on the tables using names of your favorite cars, boats, songs, cities, flowers, games x-box, video, etc., and of course… in your wedding colors.

In this wedding, the wedding was on a ferryboat on the river. The theme... boats. Each table had the name of a boat type to designate seating for the guests. Her aqua wedding color does not come in flowers, her enhancements she made, did!

When choosing your linens and flowers, make sure they compliment each other. A white tablecloth verses a black tablecloth makes a big difference in the look of your centerpiece. In this example, check out how the linen color changes the look of the centerpiece. Practice your centerpiece, place it on the color of linen you wish to use and make sure it looks like what you have in mind.

Dark flowers on black linen may not have the desired look you want.
Dark flowers disappear, and greens don't look as lush. Test everything!

The same centerpiece on white linen has a very different look.
Be sure to set up your centerpiece using the linen color on your tables.

The pictures from this summery wedding of peach, yellow and coral, are all from the same wedding. The linens added lots of color to the room which adds to the ambiance of the event. Here are more examples of how the color of linens, table runners and the napkins add to the look of the room and help make your flowers stand out.

Centerpieces Made Easy

How you display your napkin whether you fold your napkin or drape it, place the napkin on the plate or off the plate, stand up a folded napkin or display the napkin in your goblets will add to the over-all look of the reception area. Making a little décor for the napkin would add the personal touch and color.

Placing a table runner of lace, satin, burlap, organza or a variety of other materials, would add color and to the over-all look of your reception room or area. Table runners are easy to make or rent. If you use a table runner, make sure you practice the look of flowers on the color of the runner. Practicing could save you from being disappointed on the day of the event. There are rental options and your event coordinator or a party rental store should be able to help show you some samples.

With a Plan, Preparation and Practice ...

.....You Can Do It!

So How Much Will You Save?

So how much will you save? In general, you should save around 30% to 75% doing it yourself.

For example, let's assume you went out and interviewed three florists and received a quote from all of them. The general rule of thumb is to add the three quotes together, and then divide the result by 3. This will give you an average amount to use as your retail total.

Now take your average amount, and multiply by .3 (30%). Then take that same average once more and multiply by .75 (75%). This is the range of money that you can SAVE by acting as your own florist. Here's an example with numbers:

Florist #1	$2100		Quote #1
Florist #2	$1850		Quote #2
Florist #3	$2000		Quote #3
	Total	$5950	Adding the three quotes together

Florist Average	$1983	$5950 divided by 3
30% Savings	$595	$1983 multiplied by .30 (30%)
75% Savings	$1487	$1983 multiplied by .75 (75%)

Your Cost	$496 to $1388 (in this example)*

*We have to say it but none of our prices anywhere in the book includes any sales tax.

So by acting as your own florist you can have a nearly $2,000 wedding for somewhere in-between $500 to $1400! Again it all depends on what you do.

So why do florist have to charge what they do?
    1. The florist is in business with real business expenses including rent, refrigeration, gas, etc.
    2. They do everything regarding the flowers for you including set-up.
    3. A good florist possesses the knowledge to make your wedding the best it can be.

There can be a lot of physical work, but the creative talent is what you are really paying for just as in hiring the best chef, best mechanic or trusted contractor. You pay for their knowledge, experience and problem solving talents. But with a little guidance, you can also possess the basic knowledge to make your centerpieces outstanding.

It is our opinion to leave your Wedding Party flowers to the professionals however. They do bouquets, boutonnières and corsages professionally and there is a technique to making them. In very general terms, the wedding party flowers usually average in the $500 - $1500 range depending on the flowers chosen, number of people in the party, etc.

Tips and Preparation

Prior Planning, Preparation, & Practice equals Perfect!... <u>Practice, Practice and Practice</u>

Planning the simplest details will allow you to be concerned only about getting ready for your special day and to remember every moment. Those moments should be exciting with the bridesmaids, doing makeup, your hair being done and putting on your beautiful wedding dress.

The memories should <u>not</u> include, a hectic unorganized event sprinkled constantly with your helpers inundating you with questions of "what-do-we-do-now?" So let's start with some basic ideas!

A good idea is to practice... and maybe practice some more. This one simple bit of advice could be what makes the difference in your event. Write down exactly how you want it to look by using table and room diagrams for your set-up crew (included in our Appendix C for the common size tables). Take a picture and include it with your instructions. Leave nothing to chance, guess or assumption.

We have an example of two tables; the first is a 60-inch round table and the second a 72 inch round.

60 inch Round Table
Seats 8-10 people

Using our diagrams in Appendix C, you can plan the space around your centerpiece. Notice the difference in space between the two tables. Our diagrams will show your helpers how you want your set-up to look on the tables.

72 inch Round Table
Seats 10-12 people

Practice will also give you a time value. As with everything else in life, generally the more you practice, the better you will get. The time to actually make the centerpiece will get better too! Once you have a comfortable time in making the design, multiply that time by the number of centerpieces, and you will have the estimated time needed to make all the centerpieces. For example, a centerpiece using several stems of fresh flowers can easily take on average of 30-60 minutes each. If you have 15 tables, it would take up to 15 hours to do all the centerpieces, not including shopping, prep time, or set up of design space, etc.

Always add some time... You will get interrupted and have to take breaks. If the time frame estimated does not sound feasible, try a simpler, less complex design and practice... or get more dependable help!

This is so important. If you have helpers, make sure they understand your expectations. Have a practice session including the helpers that will have the responsibility for the set up on the day of the event. They will learn what they will be responsible for and how to do the final set-up of your centerpiece.

Water

A critical component to keeping your centerpieces looking fresh and long lasting is having enough water for the flowers to stay hydrated. **Another good idea is always use bottled water.** Tap water may have chemicals that can harm your flowers… especially a flower with delicate and thin petals.

Using hard water can show up in your petals appearing "burned" or discolored. In addition, if water will be used and seen by your guests (In our chapters, Floating Flowers…So Easy or Floating Candles …Vases Votives & Blooms) using bottled water will ensure the water will stay absolutely crystal-clear in your centerpieces. You have worked too hard to let the hard or impure water spoil the look of your centerpiece.

The Recipe for the Centerpieces- *Once* the practice session is over and you have selected the centerpiece, you will have a total number of the flower stems, greenery, and supplies needed for each centerpiece. This will be the "recipe" for your centerpiece. Your order will be based on the recipe multiplied by the number of centerpieces needed. Following the recipe, will keep your centerpieces evenly designed.

Temperature

Temperature is very important to your flowers. Do not place your flowers in a refrigerator or a cooler that is below <u>40 degrees Fahrenheit (5 degrees C)</u>. Extreme temperatures either hot or cold will turn your flowers black or cause them to wilt. If you decide to use the refrigerator for the storage of your flowers, do not store any type of fruit with the flowers. Fruit emits ethylene gas which will ruin your flowers. While working on flowers a temperature of 65-70 degrees Fahrenheit (18-21 degrees C) is ideal. A cool room or garage would be excellent for keeping the flowers before the wedding.

Floral Foam

To soak the floral foam, using five gallon buckets work great. The buckets need to be chemical free if used for the flowers or the floral foam (Chemicals linger and will affect your flowers). Clean the buckets with water and a few drops of household bleach, wash the sides of the bucket, and then rinse well. Fill the container about half to two thirds full of bottled water mixing in a floral preservative for better flower life. Set the floral foam on top of the water and let it soak on its own. Do NOT push it down in the water… the ***floral foam will and MUST soak on its own.*** It takes only a few minutes. Pushing the floral foam underwater doesn't make the floral foam soak faster, but would create an air pocket in the center of the floral foam causing a dry area. This would not allow the flowers that are inserted in the dry area to have water, quickly reducing the life of the flower.

Flowers in General

There are some basic fundamentals you should be aware of when working with flowers.
1. First, flowers can be expensive, fragile and require special care. When deciding your flower vendor, read the reviews or recommendations. For example, is it worth buying from a vendor, even though they have the lowest cost, when the reviews say their delivery over all is poor? Ask the vendor what the requirements are, any specific instructions for care, if they provide any floral preservative, what the seasonal flowers would be for your event season, the minimum order requirement and of course… the cost and if the delivery is included.
    a. Whether you buy from a retail store, the internet or a wholesaler, you will order in bulk. In the floral industry it is known as a "bunch".
    b. The number of stems in a "bunch" will vary. For example a bunch of Roses may have 25 stems while a bunch of Gerberas will have 10 stems.

c. Each stem will have either one bloom or an expected range of blooms on the stem. For example, a Rose stem has one bloom (the rose head) but a stem of Alstroemeria may have 3 to 5 blooms.
   d. This will be important in your design, planning and ultimate costs. If you are not knowledgeable in this area, ask your vendor what to expect for a bloom count and how many stems in a bunch for the type of flowers you want to purchase.
2. Do a "test order" from the floral vendor you have chosen. **Practice** with your design and see how your flowers last. Some flowers are more fragile, and some are heartier than others… and all require special care.
3. The required time for flowers to open maximizing their look, is not all the same. It's possible you will need to have them arrive on different days. Ask your vendor what they recommend for the flowers you are choosing. You want your flowers to be at their maximum beauty during your event. You need to allow time for the flowers to open and the time needed for you and your helpers to make the centerpiece. For your event, you may want to order an extra bunch or two of the flowers you will use the most, including an extra bunch of your filler flower.
4. Consider your time-line for preparation.

Buying and Cleaning Your Flowers

If you choose to buy from a local flower wholesaler or an online vendor, your flowers will come wrapped in plastic or heavy paper. They will not appear as they would in the retail floral environment. In a wholesale environment, you will have rows and rows of flowers to pick from.

Be careful not to drip water from the flowers you pick on other flowers. Those water drippings can ruin those flowers for others. Be sure to check for brown spots on your flowers.

Cleaning Flowers is important for the life of the flower, and your success. Follow the step-by-step instructions in this chapter for optimal life of your flowers.

Once you buy your flowers you will need to "clean" them. Wear protective gloves during this phase. It will make the cleaning easier on your hands. You don't want any cuts on your hands on your wedding day.

Cleaning flowers simply means to:

1. Take each flower stem and strip away unwanted leaves and thorns (if any).
2. Giving each stem an angled fresh-cut, cutting off an inch of the stem's end.
3. And placing the now "clean" stem in a sanitized bucket of clean fresh cool water with flower preservative.

The amount of leaves to take off the stem varies. It is up to you how much of the leaves you intend to use. However, **leaves should not be in the water at all**. Leaves when sitting in water will cause bacteria to grow. Bacteria can shorten the life of the flower quickly. If you see leaves fall in the water pull them out immediately.

Flower Preparation

The clock starts ticking on your flowers the moment they are delivered or you pick them up from your supplier. If at all possible, go immediately to your work space and clean the flowers.

Flower preparation is a very important step in the process of your centerpieces. Flowers require special care to ensure their life, look and longevity. The freshness of your flowers will be seen in your centerpieces.

Step 1.. Prepare the containers of water to put the flowers in. Buckets work great and we typically recommend 5-gallon buckets, but ultimately the length flower stem will determine the bucket size. To be absolutely certain your flowers are maintained at their best, clean your containers with tap water and a few drops of household bleach. Then rinse thoroughly. This step kills any bacteria in the container that can shorten the life of your flowers and ruin them. This step could be done before you pick up the flowers or they arrive. Saves some time and you can get ahead a little. Vases can be used for smaller or more fragile flowers like mini calla lilies, tulips or orchids.

Step 2.. Fill your containers about half to two-thirds with bottled water. Although a floral preservative is optional, it is a good idea to use it. A floral preservative not only provides nutrients for your flowers longevity, it can help to keep any bacteria from growing.

Step 3.. Unwrap all your flowers and lay them on your work table being very careful not to bruise or damage the blooms of your flowers. Carefully remove the protective wrapping, twist-ties, rubber bands or string from the flowers. Don't tear into the wrapping but rather use scissors or a sharp knife also being careful not to let the sharp blade stab or poke the blooms or petals. For example, white or light colored roses bruise very easily.

We're using roses in our example. Roses can be one of the most difficult and time consuming to clean.

Step 4.. Cleaning your flowers. This is the process of removing the unwanted leaves or thorns, giving the stems a fresh-cut and placing in the water. If you are using roses, mums, or any flowers with leaves, you want to strip the leaves starting about one-third the way down the stem from the flower bloom. On most flowers, like Stock or Mums, it's a fairly easy and fast process. You simply pull the unwanted leaves off, give a fresh-cut to the end of the stem (about an inch), and put the stem in the water. Gerberas are great... no leaves, just give them a fresh-cut.

When cleaning roses
using a "rose stripper" is the best way
to remove the thorns and leaves from a rose stem.
This is a hand held tool that surrounds the stem. You squeeze the tool
firmly; pull the stripper down the stem "stripping" the leaves and thorns
off the stem as you pull. Be careful not to squeeze too tight.
Scraping the skin of the rose will not allow the rose to hydrate the way
it should and it will shorten the life of the rose.

These thorns need to be removed in the "cleaning" process for easier and safer handling while designing your centerpieces. Use caution handling roses, thorns can hurt the fingers!

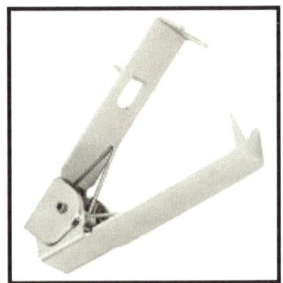

Do NOT try cleaning roses using just your bare hands! Gloves can prevent thorns scraping up your hands. You can get this Rose Stripper at most craft stores or a floral wholesaler.

Most flowers, such as the Stock pictured right, it is a fairly easy and fast process. Just pull the leaves off and give an angled fresh cut off the end of the stem.

Warning!
Always wear your gloves cleaning flowers.
You wouldn't want to come this far and have a cut on your hands for your wedding day!

Laying all your flowers out flat across your work table will make it easier to keep track of what stems you already have cleaned.

Lastly …The end of the flower stem dries out quickly and without a fresh-cut to the stem, your flower **can not** drink water. Imagine the stem is like a straw. If there is something blocking the opening of a straw at the bottom, then no water can be drawn up the straw. This is true with the flower stem.

Simply cut about an inch off the end of the stem on an angle with your floral knife or floral scissors exposing the maximum surface area of the stem to the fresh water. Quickly (use the 5 second rule) place the fresh-cut stem in the prepared container (bucket, etc.) already prepared with bottled water and flower preservative. Fresh cut all stems. This step allows the flower to "drink" and hydrate. Allow your flowers to fully hydrate by sitting at least two hours before using. If you can let them sit overnight, that would be even better.

Store your flowers in a cool place. Depending on the time of year a garage or patio would work. With warmer temperatures an air conditioned room might be necessary. Flowers still require care after you buy them. You want to be sure they will look beautiful for you and your guests. Following the steps for the care of the flowers will ensure the life and beauty of the flower.

Transporting Your Flowers

Transporting your arrangements is a very important part of your success. Most centerpieces can be completed at your home worktable and transported ready for setup on your reception tables. If you are choosing a centerpiece that is designed on site, transport the vases in their original boxes (if possible), modified boxes or wrap the vases in bubble wrap to avoid breakage. If you are choosing an arrangement that is pre-arranged, make sure your flowers don't crush each other. Make a towel ring for the flowers to sit in around the base of the arrangement (not too deep). This will help the flowers not to shift and will protect them at the same time. Cushion with crumpled paper, towels, sheets, or something you have at home that can be washed or thrown away. It is not necessary to purchase anything special. Avoid the flowers touching each other if possible.

A large vehicle is important for transport with as much flat area as possible. If you need more than one car, you'll need to plan for another volunteer who can help. Drive slower and take your time. Don't brake fast or late, go slow turning and going over bumps. The last thing you need is to ruin all your work by having arrangements fly off the seat because there wasn't enough time for a smooth stop or took a turn too fast.

Planning Your Time

Designing with fresh flowers is in essence, a last minute production. Most of the centerpiece designing and final preparations are in the last two days and even more in the last 12 to 18 hours. The time needed to produce your arrangements will vary with the choice of centerpiece and your comfort level with the design. It is so important to calculate and plan. When planning the event activities, regarding your centerpieces, your biggest error would be not having enough time to do your centerpieces the way you envision

With practice and knowing the time it takes to make your design, when the day arrives to do your centerpieces, you will be organized and know exactly what to do.

Make a List of Supplies

With each design there is a list of supplies needed for the arrangement. Many of the supplies are available online or in craft stores. We have tried to keep it simple so that finding the supplies should not be difficult (we have listed some of the suppliers we have used, or referred to, in our Appendix D at the end of the book). The cost should be calculated before purchasing anything in quantity.

You need to know the cost of your centerpiece before you start. We have tried to estimate the cost of each centerpiece, but your cost will vary depending on the vendors you choose. The cost of the flowers probably will be the greatest variance. Do your research online and locally to find what would work best for you. Keep in mind many wholesalers will sell to you at retail plus any sales tax. This can expand your choices greatly.

Decide Where Your Workspace Will Be

Figure out where you will design your centerpieces. It needs to be somewhere that will provide the room needed to spread out and work efficiently. A garage or patio is a great location as long as it is shaded and relatively cool.

Water and the flowers do create a mess! The green leaves you take off the stems will leave green marks on your floor if not cleaned up right away. So a pretty kitchen might not be the perfect place unless you protect the floor with an inexpensive tarp!

For a design table, you can use an 8 foot folding table on cement blocks, or use an old door on saw horses, plywood also works, so improvise. The reason for the cement blocks is to raise the table to a comfortable working height because you will be mostly standing.

Most people have something they can use or borrow without buying anything new.

Greens For Your Centerpiece

For the beginner, common greens would be Pittosporum, Tree Fern, Springerii, or Plumosa. Pittiosporum works very well for that web-like support we will use in designing. If you look at the Pittiosporum closely there is a "branchy web" or a radial spoke-like look. This works well for holding flowers in place in an arrangement by inserting the stem through the "web" (see our chapter *When a Bud Vase... Is Not Just a Bud Vase*).

Pittosporum has many smaller stems on a single larger stem. We can create smaller "sprig-like" stems out of the larger stem making them easier to work within designs like in the chapter, *Ring of Flowers*.

Greenery, like Pittosporum, can come in solid green or a variegated leaf. It is commonly used for landscaping and could be growing in your yard. A great way to save money! There are many types of greenery in landscaping that can be used, but here again it is imperative you practice using it first.

Cut a sample from the greenery you intend to use and give it a fresh-cut at the desired length, then put it in water quickly. Watch the greenery over a couple of days and see how it holds up in water. Again test, and re-test. Many plants simply are not good for designing as they wilt or die quickly and certainly wouldn't last for your event.

Test your greens both in water and in the floral foam if you are considering one of the centerpieces using the floral foam. Floral foam doesn't allow the greenery to draw in water the same way a vase of water would. You need to know if the greenery requires more water to keep hydrated than the floral foam allows. It is the difference between fresh or wilted greens.

Here are a few examples of greenery commonly used in arrangements.

Green Pittosporum   Variegated Pittosporum   Plumosa   Sprengerii   Tree Fern

Greens, such as Tree Fern work well in vase arrangements like a bud vase. One stem can create fullness and the stem is very thin, fitting nicely into the small opening of some bud vases.
Plumosa and Sprengerii is more like a ferny vine with length. Good for draping in tall arrangements, a ceremonial arch topper or a head table arrangement.

The Filler Flower and Finishing Touches… The finishing touches could be adding the filler flower for a garden look. The filler flower is exactly how it is described; it fills in space in the arrangement and can add more interest. Examples of commonly used filler flower would be Wax Flower, Misty Blue (white and pink also) Baby's Breath, just to name a few.

Wax Flower   Blue Status   White Status   Misty   Baby's Breath   Berries   Queen Anne's Lace

Each of the filler flowers have a stem with smaller "branchy" stems that can be cut apart for the perfect touch of contrast. From one stem, you will have several mini stems to use in your arrangement. As with anything you purchase they have different costs. Practicing will give you exactly the look and the amount of flowers you will need for your design's "recipe".

Adventure Shopping … Is Part of the Adventure in Planning an Event!

If you are deciding on glass vases, candleholders or votives, an idea would be to go to thrift stores and see what you can find. Your centerpieces don't all have to look alike. For instance, a vintage theme is a popular look and thrift store is the perfect place to start shopping. Having different sizes and shapes of glass can add to the interest of your centerpiece and the enhancements around the arrangement. The glass can also be used for floating candles.

What is your significant advantage? The cost would be much much less than buying new glass or paying a retail price. For example, while we were out one day, we drove by a thrift store and decided to put our recommendation to the test.

We decided to see what we could find… and here it is. We had planned to have varying heights of glass in groupings. Each table would have 3 vases and 6 votives. The three vases would vary in size and shape. We found different styles of glass, enough to do 2 or 3 tables. We put the glass in the dishwasher and it is now clean ready to go. Adventure Shopping may take several trips and at several thrift stores. If you are a shopper you will love this part of the planning!

Here is a look at the basic set up we are going to use, three vases in the center with 6 votives around the taller vases. Total cost for all glass = $6.91

Tip!
When you go Adventure Shopping, have a list of all the areas you want to decorate. Head Table, Bar Area, Buffet Table, Cake Table, Photo Booth, Cocktail Tables, etc. When you see a unique piece of décor… it maybe exactly what will accent that area perfectly!
You never know what you may find!

OK… what did I pay for this beautiful bowl? $3.99!
This was definitely a bonus! We love what we find. We will use this dish for a head table piece!

Dependable People are Needed!

Many friends and family will offer to help, but **choose carefully those who will help with the flowers.** Your centerpieces are an important part of your day and need to look the best for the wedding reception. A last minute cancelation of your planned helpers would certainly add to your stress level. Make the responsibility of your plan clear, and it may eliminate those who don't want the responsibility or it will make your volunteer feel more of value. So choose carefully.

If your helper(s) are also creative it is a plus! Include them in the practice session of making the centerpiece. If you have 2 to 4 people, it will reduce the time spent doing centerpieces by using a production line. Production line work will be helpful if you are planning to do a centerpiece that has several steps in designing your centerpiece.

Production Line Work

First, line up the containers you are using for the centerpieces on your worktable. The best worktable set-up would allow you and your helpers to walk around the table working on the arrangements one "production" step at a time. With identical or near identical centerpieces, making them is a simple process… Completing one-step at a time, this example of production work could be used in our chapter *Start With the Basics… Make It Your Own!*

First complete step one in the design you have chosen, such as cutting the soaked floral foam to fit the container and placing the floral foam into the container. When all your containers are double checked to ensure the floral foam is snuggly in place, then move on to step two. Loose floral foam that falls out in the middle of designing would not be good.

Second, if your floral foam is not fitting snug in your container, step two maybe to tape the floral foam in the container using floral adhesive tape. Encircle the floral foam and container with the tape holding the floral foam in place. This step is only for containers that will be hidden inside another vase or container, concealing the adhesive tape. Continue with all containers.

Third, choose the first flower you want to use as your primary flower or main flower. Measure the flower's stem to the length needed for the design. Give a fresh-cut, and then insert the stem into the floral foam. Insert all the primary flowers (for example, in our chapter *Start With the Basics...Make It Your Own,* it was six flowers). Repeat this step in each centerpiece. In checking your work, the centerpieces should be close in appearance. If you are making 15 centerpieces, you will do step one 15 times before moving on to step two.

Continue on to the next step by adding the flowers into your design the instructions call for. Complete this step on all centerpieces before moving on. Re-check your work before you proceed to the next step. This will help keep your design true, and will save you time in the long run. Trying to correct a design after completed, is much harder.

An example of designing an arrangement in a production line with some helpers would be:

If you have a helper, they would follow you doing Step 2 after you complete Step 1. You would then do Step 3, and your helper would do step 4, and so on. The more help you have the less steps each person will have to do.

Practice by doing one centerpiece before your work party. You will then have a good idea how the design goes together, which will help with direction when doing them in a production line. Completing your centerpieces in a step-by-step production line process will be more efficient and faster than completing a centerpiece individually one at a time. It gives all your centerpieces a more consistent look and frankly, it's more fun as social get-together. Don't forget to take pictures at the practice session. They will be needed by the set up crew for your wedding day, and then one goes into the bride's memory book.

Setting Up Your Centerpieces at Your Reception Site

Assume you have to be self-supporting and will not have any help from the venue. Make sure you have all the tools and the helpers you will need to complete the task of set up. Find out from the venue coordinator where to park your vehicle(s), where your workspace (or staging area) could be, and where can you store the boxes after you are done unpacking them. You need to save them for packing up after the event to take your centerpieces back home (or you could just give the centerpieces away as gifts!).

Delegate to a responsible person to be the lead in setting up and directing other helpers! Give them the extra flowers to replace any flower breakage, to place the centerpieces on the tables and to set any vases, candles, or enhancements in or around each centerpiece. They will be the ones responsible for all those little details that are so important.

Find out from your event planner if the staff at the venue will light the candles at the appropriate time, or should you have your dependable person responsible for it.

Tip!

When opening your candles from the box, check to see if
they are individually wrapped. If so, take the cellophane off; protect them by
putting a paper towel between them. This will save time on the day of the event.
When setting out the candle on the tables, take the time to stand the candlewick "up"
to make it easy to light. In addition, make sure you have at least two lighters
for your helpers to light candles 15 to 20 minutes before the guest's arrive!

Plan Ahead… Stay on Schedule…. And save money! Waiting to make your centerpieces the last day or two before the wedding can be stressful. If you are someone that can be stressed somewhat easily… this may NOT be for you. However, with this book, prior planning, preparation, and some reliable help, you will eliminate many of the problems and feel more comfortable if you decide to do your own centerpieces.

You can plan and prepare weeks ahead… Components of the centerpiece that are not perishable can be made weeks or months in advance:

- Write out your "supplies list" and finalize the "recipe" for the flower design you have chosen after you do your availability and cost research.
- Select your vendors.
- Test your flower vendor.
- Test the time it takes for your flower choice to open fully. This will determine when your flowers should arrive or be purchased. It could involve more than one day of arrival.
- Practice your design, know the time it takes. Determine the scheduled day/s for centerpiece production. By working backwards from your date, will give a good idea of a schedule. Planning out the details will go a long way to meeting your expectations on your wedding day.
- Purchase your supplies, including anything non-perishable such as silk or latex flowers that may be used in your centerpieces.
- Clean your buckets, vases, containers or glass so they are ready when your flowers arrive.
- Clean and protect vases, gems or any product you plan to use and have them ready to go.
- Reuse all product shipping boxes or make your own.
- Make any bows or loops of ribbon you may need. Poke the wire end in a piece of Styrofoam allowing the bow to stand, instead of laying the bow down.
- Make anything that is non-perishable such as a table runner, napkin décor or your wedding favors, box them up to keep them clean and ready to go.
- Organize your supplies in labeled boxes or totes that are not needed until you are on the wedding site.
- Have your work area and the supplies ready to go for when your flowers arrive.
- Don't forget to take pictures of the design set up for your helpers so they "picture it".
- Don't forget to practice making your centerpiece with your helpers. Practicing ahead of time will ensure they will know what to do on the day of your wedding… without you! You will have other things to do… **like getting ready to look beautiful for your pictures!**

Enhancements... So Many Choices

Enhance your centerpiece... with mirrors, candles, candleholders, LED lights, glitter spray, fresh or silk petals, small floating blooms, side pieces, table runners, overlays, material or napkin squares, wooden slices of a log, framed pictures, or beautiful tiles... the list is infinite! Enhancements to your centerpieces are limited only by your imagination... here is just few.

Mirrors can be found just about anywhere you look, in all shapes, sizes and price points. Here is a list of tips regarding mirrors:

Tips!

Make sure the mirror isn't scratched on the front or back. A scratched mirror can take away from the look of your centerpiece.

If possible, a beveled mirror would be preferable. A beveled mirror has a finished polished edge and is one of those details that enhance the centerpiece with very little extra cost. Beveled mirrors can be found online and at a home improvement store. We found the home improvement store was the most reasonably priced and readily available.

Clean mirrors thoroughly! Remove all dust, fingerprints and smears allowing the mirrors to reflect and sparkle!

Handle all glass with care using gloves or a lint free cloth to prevent finger prints.

Candles are a very popular choice. The glow of a candle can create a romantic, elegant mood-setting ambiance like nothing else can. Candles can compliment any look or theme you create and come in a wide variety of colors, size and price points.

Test the quality before buying quantity. The best advice is before you purchase in quantity... test the quality! We have had brides purchase hundreds of votive candles cheaply, only to find out the candles would not stay lit! The one that did stay lit lasted maybe 1 or 2 hours or less! There is a quality to candles just like any other product. Buy different kinds to test, see how long they last before you buy a large quantity of candles!

Create your look by:

- Surrounding your centerpieces with candles of different heights using candleholders. The candleholders would not have to match.

- Use different size candles: tapers, floating candles in several sizes, votives and/or pillar candles.

- Decorate your votive candleholders coordinating with your wedding theme or look. Add Bling, pearls rhinestones ribbon, crystals, glitter or something vintage.

- Floating candles can be used in cylinder vases of varied sizes and heights with floral side pieces. Use pebbles, gems or decorative rock in the bottom of the vases. See our chapter on *Floating Candles...Vases Votives & Blooms.*

- Group the vases of candles on half of your tables with flower arrangements on other tables.

The time of year of your wedding is very important! If 100-degree weather is a possibility, candles may not be the best choice because they visually project "heat".

However, there is another option. This is a glowing centerpiece using LED lights. LED lights create a glow without the heat. LED lights can also be submerged in water or the crystal gels. One significant advantage to the LED lights is they last for hours and they can be turned on and placed in your vases at set-up. You can then forget about them. These are available where party supplies are typically sold

... Or you could use both candles and the LED lights.

Your enhancements and the little décor touches is what will make your event special. Gather all the items you would like to have around your centerpieces. Practice with all the items. You may find that you have too much, or it might not look like what you envisioned.

When you find the "look", write it down, sketch it out, and take a picture or whatever works best for you. This simple step will save time and will give your helpers a great way to follow through with your plans.

Simple Enhancements

Enhancements to the centerpiece could be colorful tiles from the home improvement store, chargers under the plates or the centerpiece; a color framed mirror under the centerpiece, or a flower on the napkin… out of the box thinking could be a big hit and great look.

Table runners…

Table runners add color, texture, décor and are a wonderful enhancement. They can be any type of material and you can make them yourself. A popular look currently is burlap. A material like burlap has a texture, creates a rustic theme and comes in a variety of colors. It can easily be trimmed in lace by hot gluing the lace on the edge. Burlap will unravel easily so if there is not a preventative measure taken, you should handle it carefully.

Our examples of table runners are those that brides have chosen. As you can see as simple as they are, they add so much to the table and to the room.

Our example of the white table runner on the navy table cloth shows the only other table décor is an arrangement in the middle of the table. A runner could add the color and décor needed and may be the thing to simplify your centerpiece idea.

Do some research; compare what a runner would cost to rent verses making them. Some type of materials need a professional touch to make them look good enough for your event. Wrinkled or frayed edges will take away from your overall look. We have found table runners online, in the department stores on clearance, and of course you can rent them. Keep in mind you do not have to have them all the same color. Reverse the colors on some tables. With some research you will find a table runner that would fit your budget.

If you want to make your own runners, one idea is to use two textures and create a unique look. We show a burlap runner with a lace runner on top. This bride cut strips of material in the runner length, and then cut a lace runner slightly narrower to place on top. There was nothing on the edges, not even hems. They looked beautiful on the guest's tables. Simply done.

A slice of a wood log has also been a popular choice for an accent. The wood look goes well with the Mason jar. Follow through with the wedding color in the Mason jar by using the colored gems and colored floating or votive candles. Make this bud vase following our instructions in our chapter *When a Bud Vase... Is Not Just a Bud Vase.*

Or... Use one or two napkins representing the main wedding colors by laying them flat in the center of the table under your centerpiece.

Or... A beautiful tablecloth upgrade can fill the room with unmistakable wedding color like the teal and red color scheme.

Another option would be to use over-lays on your table cloths. This would be a sheer material on a solid table cloth. Overlays can be as elaborate as you wish. The choice of patterns, colors and design are extensive and can be rented through your linen company. This embroidered white on white overlay makes the flowers really stand out! The arrangement shown can be designed following instructions in the chapter *Rings of Beauty... Simply Done.*

Centerpieces Made Easy

Making Perfect Bows Everytime

Adding a loop of wired ribbon can represent a wedding color that may not be in flowers. Sadly not all the beautiful fashion colors are available in fresh flowers.

"Wired Ribbon" is a real easy way to add that missing color. Wired ribbon will make your life easy when it comes to making bows and using ribbon as accents. Bow making is simple when you specifically use wired ribbon. You can make the ribbon bows or loops weeks in advance, and the wire allows you to re-shape the bow just before use. A ribbon accent can bring in color, to fill-in an area of the centerpiece, is cost effective and looks beautiful! The perfect accent!

Making a Ribbon Loop is easy. Here's how to do a simple loop for an accent in color, style or support a theme.

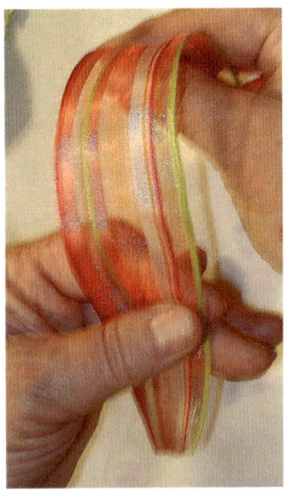
Hold ribbon end closest to your body making a loop.

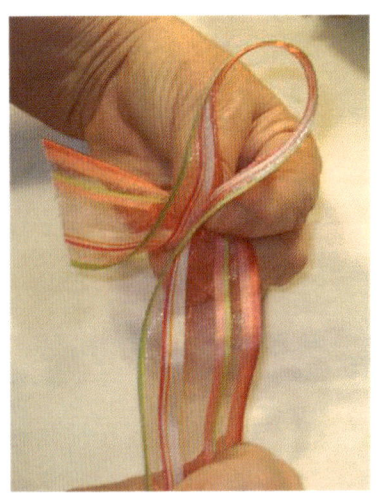
Make your loop the size you wish. Hold the loop with your thumb and index finger.

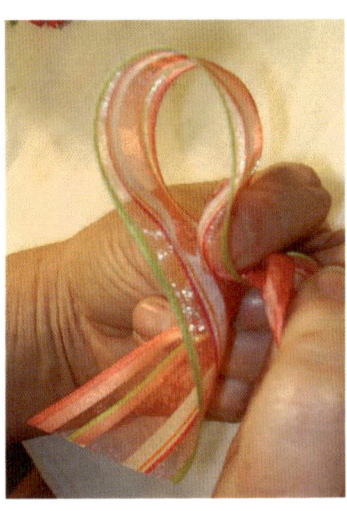
Twist the part of the ribbon below your index finger.

  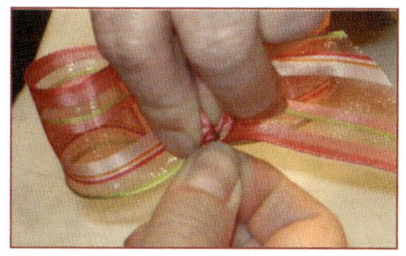

Cinch the ribbon where the twist is, making a gathering effect. Hold firmly to the gathered part of the ribbon. Then cut the tail of the ribbon as desired.

Your wire now will be placed at the gathered area of the bow. Bend your wire to make a U-shape around the twisted part of the ribbon. The ends of the wire pointing away from you.

With your fingers or pliers twist the wire tightly to hold the loop You can twist wire fairly tightly, but it can break. You will have to start over if the wire breaks.

Cut the wire to leave about 3 inches of the wire to insert into the centerpiece floral foam. Fluff the loop and arrange the tails of the ribbon. Look for any bare spots where the floral foam is showing. Tuck in the ribbon where it might be needed to fill in a space and help cover the floral foam.

Leave the length of the wire longer if you are using the bow in a bud vase. If you want more loops in your bow then keep making the loops. As you make the loop, don't forget to twist the ribbon each time you come to the center. Gradually make the loops a little bigger each time you pass the center of the bow. Keep making loops until you like the size of the bow.

Practice your bows and you will become quite good. You will be able to use your skill to make chair bows or gift table bows. You can even get a little crafty and hot glue a silk bloom or a strand of pearls into your bows. Practice on different types of ribbon. You will find wired ribbon easy to work with, and will be easiest to fluff right before the wedding.

Centerpieces Made Easy

Simple and Elegant… From Start to Finish!!!

This beautiful, simple and elegant centerpiece is easy to prepare and very budget friendly. The following instructions outline all the steps you need to make this centerpiece… and much of it can be done **weeks before** your wedding. The actual setup on the day of your wedding can be accomplished by your responsible helpers. This centerpiece is so easy that anyone with no floral experience would be able to help you the day of set-up. The best way you can effectively plan and instruct your helper(s), is to have a practice session prior to your wedding. With your written instructions and a picture of how you want it set up, you are on your way to a flawless event.

Phase 1 – Decide on Your Centerpiece

Keep in mind, all your vases don't have to be identical, but they are in this example. Make one centerpiece to actually see the finished product. In our example, we will go through the entire process for a simple yet elegant centerpiece. This centerpiece that has only four components: 1) The vase, 2) water, 3) gems, and 4) a single fresh flower of your choice. Flowers that work well would be the Gerbera, Rose, Spider Mum, Orchid, and Dahlia just to name a few.

Phase 2 – Inspect, Remove Stickers and the Cleaning of Your Vases

We're using an old door on a pair of saw horses for our work table. It could be your kitchen table.

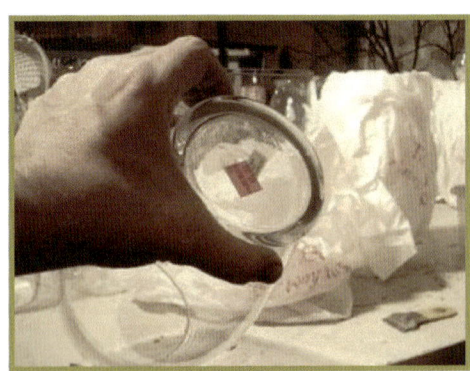

These vases were purchased at a local discount store and the clerk had individually double-bagged each vase for transport. Look at your vases when you get home. It is important that there no cracks or chips in the glass.

There may be price stickers and they need to be removed. Typically a razor scrapper will do the job quickly and cleanly. If a razor does not remove the sticky residue, then use some "Goo Gone" or rubbing alcohol on a paper towel to remove it. To thoroughly clean the inside and outside of the glass vase use paper towels and a glass cleaner

Phase 3 – Make the Boxes for Transporting or Delivering Your Centerpieces

Make your custom boxes for transporting your centerpieces. Remember that glass can become heavy, and can shift easily. You don't want to go through all of the planning and have the vases broken when you get to the venue (or in your hand!!!). Our example here is how we have transported many centerpieces and it has worked quite well. To start, you will need to find sturdy cardboard boxes in good shape with both the top and bottom; the lid needs to be deep, similar to the boxes in the picture.

With the box upside-down, draw a line around the base of the vase keeping at least a few inches between vases.

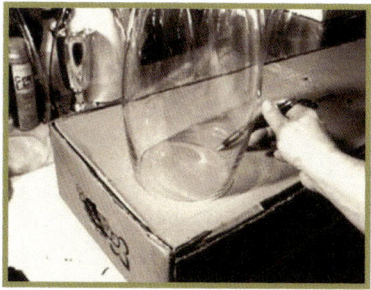

Start with the box upside-down, with the lid on. This will prevent the bottom from falling out when you lift it! Always use sharp blades for cutting (they are safer!). When cutting, make four equal distant diagonal "star" cuts, and then individually punch down the tabs. Stagger your cuts leaving 2 to 3 inches between the holes (see the picture). Punch down the "tabs", carefully to avoid ripping. Keep in mind too many rips will make the box weaker but if the cardboard rips a little, it's still workable.

Shown in picture: Using a sharp utility knife razor, make four equal distant diagonal "star" cuts and then individually punch down the tabs.

Place a vase in your box to test for sizing. You want the vase to be snug without movement. Notice the vases are staggered in the transport box.

With one completed box, you are ready to move to the next box. Once you have your shipping boxes done, and your vases stored in them, they are not only now more protected against damage but everything will begin to seem to be neater and more organized. While storing your glass, you may want to put a sheet, plastic or something over your vases that will help prevent them from getting dusty.

If you do not have both the top and bottom of good boxes, use the boxes to store the vases, wrapping each one with a towel, clean rag, sheet, etc. to provide cushion between your vases. The finished product should be a sturdy box that keeps your vases separate and prevents them from bumping each other while in transport.

Phase 4 – Transporting Materials to Site

This centerpiece can be put together on-site. Here our bride is loading up her vehicle beginning with the vases, the gems and bottled water. Once everything is loaded up, you may have a very full vehicle.

Everything should be comfortably-snug so as to avoid damage enroute. Neatness does count! The last thing you need is to have something break at this point! And don't rush driving!

Gems and vases are very heavy, take precautions not to hurt your back. Use a cart or hand truck to help carry these items to the vehicle. All the glass and gems should be clean and ready to go. You do not want anything floating in the water when it is time to pour the water in! All your time spent to clean and prepare will pay off when it comes time for the set-up.

Phase 5 – Setting Up Your Centerpieces On-Site

Assume the venue will not be able to help you in any way! You have now arrived at your venue to unload all your materials. Once you locate a staff person, ask where you can park to unload your vehicle(s), where to set-up and the best place to work would be.

Keep in mind you will need to store your boxes somewhere after the setup, so ask the venue coordinator where the best place would be. Sometimes it can be under cloth-draped tables, it could be somewhere else "in the back". In any event you will need them for repacking after the event is over.

> Stay organized and follow the plan. Also, be prepared to clean up any mess the set-up helpers make. Have a broom!

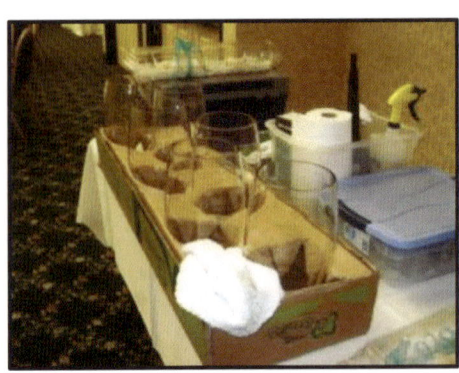

Here we are using tables at the venue that are in the hallway. Be very careful to be as neat as possible. Don't expect anyone to clean up after you. If someone at your venue is willing to help then great! But it's your responsibility so be prepared.

Our gems were left in the netting they were purchased in. We rinsed them in the netting and have not cut them open or handled them until now.

Use an old clean towel to grab the glass. Clean gloves are better. You do not want to get finger prints on your clean vase. This type of glass can be easily broken if not supported by the bottom when you handle it. Place a vase on each table with amount of gems you planned for.

Don't "tear" the netting open or gems may wind up everywhere!

Cut the netting open with a knife or scissors.

Using a knife or scissors, carefully cut open the netting and gently place the gems in the bottom of the vase.

We are using two small bags of gems per vase. Be careful not to "pour" the gems in but rather "place" them in.

Find a reference mark to help keep the water level consistent as you fill each vase with the water.

You can use anything, but here we're using the bar code on another bottle of water.

Now pour the water in the vases. You should already have decided how high the water should be in each vase from practicing in prior weeks. It is usually better to have single vases contain the same amount of water looking consistent... unless you are after a specific look.

Pour the water in the vase with a long-neck funnel. It helps control the amount water flow, prevents splashing and water spots on the inside of the vase. Also, your gems will not shift as much.

You want to be careful to not splash the inside of the vase, so using a long neck funnel works great. You can control the amount of water flow and where it goes. The last thing you want to do is soak the table linens! Water spots are not a part of your "look". A long neck funnel is available at most big box stores and auto stores.

Now we're ready for the final touches. All we need to do is place a single large Gerbera in the vase.

Note the position of the fingers holding the Gerbera.

You do not want to put any pressure on the Gerbera. If a Gerbera's petal falls out the flower can unravel.

Handle with care.

Gently take one Gerbera from your bucket of flowers and give it another fresh-cut leaving enough stem to reach the gems. Gently holding the Gerbera with thumb in the center and fingers supporting the petals, again gently and carefully place the flower in the center of the vase. We want to try and not touch the inside of the vase with our hand or fingers. Our goal is a sparkling clean glass vase.

Tip!

Gerberas can unravel! If you pull out a petal or somehow bump the Gerbera where petal(s) fall out, it might be best to replace it. Petals floating in the water would not look the best!

Notice how the stem is cut and then placed into the gems.

This will help keep the Gerbera in place.

Centerpieces Made Easy

We are now basically finished with the centerpiece!

Double check the centerpieces, wipe any fingerprints or smudges on the glass, and then place the centerpiece to the center of the table. Support the vase by the bottom holding it with a clean towel.

Phase 6 – Enjoying Your Centerpieces!

The centerpiece is now done! All that is left is to accent the centerpiece if you choose. In this case, the bride had three votive candles in matching wedding colors around the centerpiece.

This centerpiece is as simple as it can be to make and the cost is easy on the budget:

Item	Qty	Total	Source
Vase	1@ $5.00	$5.00	Thrift store, discount or craft store
Gerbera	1@ $2.00	$2.00	Local florist, big box store, wholesaler
Gems	2@ $1.00	$2.00	Discount store, dollar store
Votives Holders	3@ $0.50	$1.50	Discount store, craft store
Votive Candles (10 hour burn)	3@ $0.50	$1.50	Local craft store
Bottled Water (1 gallon)or less	1@ $1.00	$1.00	Grocery store, etc.
		$13.00	
Professional Florist Cost		$31.50	The cost difference is mostly in the choice of glass and where you buy your flowers
Your Savings Each!		**$18.50**	**Shopping and Research pays!**

There are many variations to this simple idea. Change the shape of the vase, the color of the gems, or the flower or the color of the flower. The cost is going to vary on your preference of glass and the choice of flower. Shop around!

But as you can see, for a limited budget you have many options and control of the cost with this centerpiece. When you add your special touches of the wedding favors, petals, mirrors, or your themed items, you can make it uniquely you.

We have included some variations of the same basic idea in the next chapter *Simple to do... Easy on the Budget*. If you do your research and adventure shopping, you can do this centerpiece for approximately $10.00 - $12.00. That is so much value for the look you get. At the end of the evening you can give the centerpieces as gifts to your friends and family who may have helped make your day very special.

Choose the color of the gems, flowers, and a theme that works with your wedding colors... for a centerpiece that is simple and elegant.

Simple to do... Easy on the Budget

Start with a simple idea...

Some of the prettiest centerpieces are simple in construction and design. We will help with ideas and give you options for a beautiful centerpiece while stretching the flower budget. You can combine any of these ideas to make your centerpiece.

We will give step by step instructions for each design with guide lines for planning ahead to simplify the days prior to the wedding. Following these steps will maximize the flower budget and create a wonderful centerpiece for your very special day.

Showcase your flower...

For this floating design, one or two types of flowers work best. Your primary flower (one that is about 3 inches in diameter) might be a Gerbera, Rose, Spider Mum or a Cymbidium Orchid just to name a few.

Next Choose the Container or Vase...

There are so many to choose from! Glass, ceramic, upscale plastics, brass or silver would all work beautifully. It is important to follow through with the look of the wedding. For example if you are using silver accents like ribbon, crystals, or mirrors you might consider using a clear glass or silver container for your centerpiece.

Centerpieces Made Easy

Options for Floating the Flower...

You could use clear or colored water, clear or colored crystal gels that come in a variety shapes like ice cubes, marbles or crushed ice. The crystals can be purchased premade or in a powder form. With the powder, you add water, let sit and the product forms (***read directions for disposing of the gels as some can cause plumbing problems if put down any type of plumbing or drain***). Crystal gels can also help hold your flowers in place. If water is used with a clear vase, possibly add gems, pebbles or rocks in the bottom of the vase to add interest. If the weather is warm, instead of candles, submersible LED lights are an option.

The Basic Steps...

You have picked your primary flower, the vase or container; you have decided what you would like the flower to float in; water, crystals, or clear or colored gems. All your supplies should be purchased, cleaned and ready to go.

For most of the floating flowers you could have them arrive a day or two before the event.

- **Step 1..** Clean your flowers. Gerberas make it easy because they do not have leaves (refer to flower preparation for complete flower care), next give the flower an angled fresh-cut at the bottom of the stem. Hydrate the flowers by placing them in cool clean water with some flower preservative. They should sit and "drink" for at least 2-3 hours, and overnight would even better. This centerpiece is a design that will be done on site.

    Carefully pack up everything for transport.

    Now we are ready to assemble the centerpieces on site.

- **Step 2..** Wipe the containers or vases from any dirt or dust one more time. Line up the vases or containers so that multiple centerpieces can be done at one time.

- **Step 3..** If you have decided to use gems, crystals or pebbles, place them in the bottom of your container.

- **Step 4..** Using your long-neck funnel, pour in the bottled water about an inch above the gems, polished rock or pebbles.

- **Step 5..** Cut the stem of your flower with your floral scissors or floral knife leaving the stem about 2 inches long. Quickly insert the stem into the pebbles or gems about an inch. Just enough for the flower to be gently held in place and gives the look of the flower floating.

Note: If the stem is too long and you want the flower to be lower in the vase, simply cut the stem a little shorter and reinsert into the pebbles or crystals. If you have decided to use more than one stem, repeat these steps cut and insert the flowers one at a time.

We now have the basic arrangement... Let's enhance...

Here are pictures of set ups using this very simple and basic arrangement that will look pretty and help keep the stress level low!

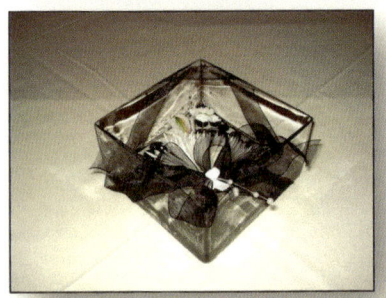  

Having a theme or being consistent in your look will tie your room together. With black and white elegance, this bride wanted a gift wrapped look. She has used the square in her centerpieces and with her cake. The cake has a bow with flower blooms tucked in for her cake top. Start with a very simple idea or theme and add your variations and enhancements.

The square glass is set off by LED submersible lights, votive candles, or the floating candles inside the square glass. If you are considering using a "non-fresh" flower, try floating some latex flowers (has a rubbery feel). Your centerpiece will work best with latex or silk flowers that look realistic (make sure they are non-flammable with candles in the container). Many glass shapes and sizes are available. Here again, practicing will let you see what you like best... fresh or faux.

These centerpieces show the variation in glass, placement of flowers, candles, use of color and the use of LED lights in the clear gems. In your practice run, move and experiment with all your items that make up your centerpiece until you find exactly what and how you like it… then take a picture to remind yourself and for your helpers the day of set up!

This is very similar to the centerpiece we just finished. The vase is approximately 12 inches tall giving the centerpiece some height. We used fresh Gerberas, clear gems and both LED lights and candles.

This centerpiece keeps on expanding with a few more Gerberas, napkin floral touch, a Gerbera in a votive holder, candles and a little picture frame with a special picture.

A Citrus Fruit Arrangement... Summer Time

A Citrus Fruit arrangement is colorful and has a refreshing look... especially if yours is a summer wedding! Your summer wedding look can be beautifully cool and fresh!

This venue provides a perfect setting for the colors this bride chose. With the citrus she used Green, Purple, and Orange in the midst of the garden courtyard.

Courtyard D'ORO, Old Sacramento, California
Photos by Alba Fiore- Dawn Spinella

Decide your colors. Are they Lemony Yellow, Perfect Peach or Sage Green? Then maybe this arrangement is an idea for you! Simple to do and wonderfully colorful! This could be an activity for all your bridesmaids a couple of days before of your wedding.

A clear glass cylinder vase 6 inches tall and 8 inches in diameter is nestled in a Pedestal vase filled with sliced and whole oranges, lemons and limes with Diamond shaped faux crystals sprinkled in the arrangement.

This centerpiece can be done quite easily with your helpers slicing the fruit a day to two before your event.
For a last minute floral touch, tuck in a few fresh flower blooms on top of the fruit.

First... Practicing this arrangement will give you the amount of citrus needed for the vases you have chosen. You can use different style and shapes of glass vases on each table.

Second... Slice or quarter the fruit as you wish, or use a combination. Use some fruit whole, like the limes shown in the picture at the end of this chapter. The whole fruit is easier to use with the slices tucked in and you may find it a great look.

Third... Place the fruit in the glass showing the fruit at different angles with the **diamond crystals** filling in the gaps. Avoid simply dumping the fruit in your arrangement. Placing the sliced fruit in your vase at varied angles around the whole fruit will be more eye-appealing.

See our example picture for placement ideas. If you choose not to have the middle vase as shown, use whole fruit to hold and fill in the center placing the sliced fruit around the edges.

Fourth... Decide what you might want to place on your tables around the arrangement of fruit. We made some enhancements for the tables by using a decorated orange. We made a bow, and stuck the wire in the orange to hold the bow in place. Glue in a name card, silk bloom, rhinestones, and pearls or continue your theme. To make the orange "stand-up" or not roll, stick 3 corsages pins in the bottom creating little feet. A decorated orange is a great way to identify the table for your guests.

Summer can be warm, so not to add more heat with candles, maybe place an LED light for the glow in votive holders with crystal gels. Another idea, place a cut flower in a little vase or a bloom in a votive holder around your citrus creation.

The colors and setting can be as creative as you wish. The use of color in the courtyard setting has been done extremely well.

This bride added purple to the mix. Purple table cloths, sage green overlays, orange and purple flowers with a vintage candleholder. We also placed the decorated orange at the place setting and made it a place card holder. The decorated orange identified the table where the guest would be seated and provided more color.

Each table had a slightly different arrangement. Guests love to see something different when attending weddings and this setting gave the guest a reason to keep on looking around the room.

A votive holder with an LED light instead of candles inserted in crystal gels looks wonderful! Don't be afraid to experiment, and practice!

Tall vases filled with whole oranges, lemons, limes and diamond shaped crystals filling in the gaps, give a cool and icy look. Fruit, sliced or not, is perfect for a warm summer day wedding. This idea is so easy to plan and create for any event.

Flowers with... Citrus Slices

This is a simple, yet pretty way to have a refreshing look, especially in the warmer weather temperatures. Adding a slice of citrus with your favorite flowers offer color, a cool look, and is so simple to do. You can add as many flowers as you wish and it can be done in silks with faux slices of fruit. Even faux is fun to do!!!

Step 1.. Select two containers that will fit inside each other. We have two plastic square containers that fit inside each other with about 1/3 of an inch of space between the two square containers on each side.

You can see the space where the limes slices need to fit between our two containers.

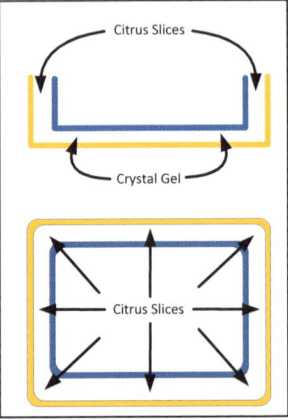

Step 2.. We have chosen to use fresh lime slices. Cut the limes (or your choice of citrus) into thin slices. The thickness should be just enough to fit in the outside space between the two squares. To test, cut 4 slices and slide one slice between the squares on each side. This holds the inside container in place, then you will know how thin or thick to cut each slice of citrus. Adjust if necessary.

Step 3.. Continue to slide limes in the space filling in all sides till you have the desired look.

Step 4.. If you have decided to use crystal gels, then fill in the spaces around the slices. If not, nothing more is required. If you use the fresh citrus slices adding water would turn the water cloudy before the event was over.

Step 5.. Pour water into the **inside** square. This is where your flowers will be designed.

Centerpieces Made Easy

Tip!
Transporting your arrangements is something always to keep in mind, so you may only want to fill the container about half way. Pour enough water in the container to ensure the flowers will be in at least in 2-3 inches of water. When you are ready to place on your guests tables, then add more water. Using a funnel helps as you do not want to spill water over your beautiful linens... water spots on your linens are not part of your look. Your flowers need to last several hours so water is very important. Once you get to the venue, remember to add water. Water may have spilled in transport.

Step 6.. Choose your "web-like" flower or greenery to help hold the flowers in place. Give the stem a fresh cut, and insert into the inside square vase. Use two stems of Hydrangea if you like it fuller, it will also help to make it easier for your flowers to stay in place. Now for the main flower, we chose the ever popular Mini Gerbera.

Step 7.. Give the flower a fresh-cut and leave the stem long enough to reach the bottom of the vase. Remember the vase is only half-full for easier transport, so the flower stem needs to be long enough to be in the water a good couple of inches.

Add as many flowers as you wish. Write down the number of flowers you have used. At the end of this chapter, we show a variation of this arrangement using lemons and Hydrangea in the center.

The Finish…
Add your enhancements around the arrangement.
Ideas we used included the napkin
with décor, votive candle, mirror, and a silk
Orchid bloom on the plate. Now…
Add your ideas for the perfect touch!

Centerpieces Made Easy

Do you love Hydrangea and want to let it show? Here are a couple of examples using Hydrangea and lemons. We used the color scheme of sage green, the Hydrangea blue and of course lemon yellow. Little touches like a lemon next to the arrangement brings out more color for very little cost. Adding a flower bloom on the edge of the guest's plate is a detail that can help tie your look together. In our example you can compare the look of the flower bloom on and off the plate. If you plan to use chargers, have the chargers on the table ready to go, add the flower bloom to the edge.

See our chapters on *Enhancements and* or *Napkin Décor* for more ideas and pictures.

Hydrangea and Lemons… or Limes! This arrangement was made following the instructions in this chapter. We used three stems of Hydrangeas, lemons instead of limes, and nothing else (except water).

So Easy… So Pretty!

When a Bud Vase... Is Not Just a Bud Vase

A bud vase is a simple design, easy to make, and fun to enhance for your table décor. When choosing your vase, a common mistake is to choose one that has too large of an opening.
The bud vase in the picture has a 1 inch opening.

The bud vase shown has a rose, greenery, filler and a bow arranged in a black vase. This bride's colors were red and black. Notice how the colors were incorporated through the simple use of a red rose and a black vase. You can then enhance with mirrors, candles, petals, or something a little more of personal interest.

The Very Classy Calla Lily

This centerpiece stands tall in a silver ceramic vase, large white Callas, accented with greenery, white Alstroemeria blooms, and a sheer silver ribbon. This bride's color scheme was an aqua, white and silver. Since flowers don't come in all the beautiful designer colors, Aqua napkins, Aqua trim on the guest place cards, and aqua chair bows brought the entire color scheme together. The ceramic vase was not silver to begin with, but a can of non-flammable silver spray paint customized the vase perfectly!

A Calla Lily designed in this clear vase with Curly Willow, large leaves, red gems in the bottom of the vase, and a branch of red leaves provides the bride with her wedding colors of red and brown. Fresh Curly Willow is pliable, easy to work with, giving the arrangement added interest and its own "personality".

An added touch for this arrangement could be some moss, a stem of grapes, twine loops, or a loop of burlap... the possibilities are limitless! This vase has 1 1/2 inch opening allowing the bud vase to hold slightly larger stems. Practicing will get you familiar with the design and amount of product you will need.

Designing a vase arrangement and getting the flowers to stay in place is usually the hard part. We can help with that. Floppy flowers just do not look good, and they do not transport well either. With this design, the vase opening is 1 to 2 inches. This is important when starting to design your flowers in the vase. The bigger the opening the more product needed. It can be odd looking if the quantity of flowers is not in balance with the size of the vase.

Choosing the filler flower, greenery and branches are also important to the over all look of your flowers. Here we have used a dark red leafy branch with Curly Willow, Bear Grass, and Lemon Leaves. Making loops out of Curly Willow is a wonderful focal point. Twine, burlap, Lotus Pod or maybe dried leaves are all possibilities for something interesting in your arrangement. Our examples of bud vases show the simple to a little more elaborate. They all follow the same method of design.

Another option for your vase arrangement would be silk flowers which can be done quite easily. You can mix silk flowers with fresh greenery to give it the fresh look. Making your centerpiece out of silks allows you to prepare weeks ahead of time. You have so much control of time when you use silks. The appearance of silk or latex (that rubbery feel) flowers have come a long way and can look quite realistic. We have mixed in latex flowers when the fresh flower wasn't available and no one could tell it was a "non-fresh" flower! They also are not as fragile as fresh flowers.

Practicing will be the way to determine what you like best and what your comfort level would be.

We will begin with a basic bud vase. Easy as 1, 2, and... 3!

Choosing the size of your vase is important. A couple of ideas to consider would be 1) the size of the opening of the vase because it will determine the quantity of flowers needed and 2) the height of the vase with flowers. The composition of the vase is whatever your preference would be.

For this demonstration we have chosen a clear glass vase with an embedded design that stands 8 inches tall with an opening of ½-inch. This is very small opening, good for two or three stems, but excellent for the beginner. Once you have the idea for the basic arrangement, you can expand to larger vases and designs, and put your own flair to it!

Before starting, remember you should have already cleaned and hydrated your flowers (See the Chapter on Flower Preparation).

   One... Use a stem of greenery to make a "web" in your vase. Pittosporum works very well due to the web-like stem. You could also use a stem of a full flower like Hydrangea that has a natural web-like-bloom to help hold your flowers in place. For our demo we are using one stem of Hydrangea.

To determine how long the stem should be in the vase, hold up the flower to the vase. The length of the stem should be long enough to reach the bottom of the vase with the bloom of the hydrangea ending up at the lip of the vase. Make an angled fresh cut to the stem and put the stem in the vase quickly. This allows maximum water to the flower bloom.

Two... Now take your next flower and repeat this step. We are using a Gerbera for our second flower. We want to hold the flower up to the vase to gauge the height. This is going to be up to you as far as the height of your centerpiece. You may have a personal preference to the height of the bud vase. For a good balance, a basic rule of thumb is your vase should equal about a third of the total height of the arrangement. It can vary, but to start it is a good rule to follow.

The length of the stem should go to the bottom of the vase and still maintain the height desired. Fresh cut the flower to your desired length, and then insert the flower through the Hydrangea (or "web") in the top center.

Repeat with your third flower. Again, gauge the length (should be shorter than the previous flower), do a fresh-cut, then insert into the vase through the "web" of flower or greenery.

If you use Hydrangea, the leaves can sometimes be turned inward or convex. Hold the leaf with your fingers behind the leaf and your thumbs on the top of the leaf's edge. Gently push with your fingers, to turn the leaf out.

Add the filler flower, bow or décor of your choice.

and... Three!!! Ribbon can be elegant, fun, vintage or whatever look you may want. Since flowers do not always come in the colors of the wedding, ribbon can add the missing color. Ribbon can be "wired" meaning a thin wire manufactured in the edge of the roll of ribbon allowing for easy handling. A wired ribbon is easier to use for many reasons. It holds its shape, can be fluffed if messed up, can be made weeks ahead of time ready for use, and is great for a beginner or the expert. Two small loops of ribbon (See Chapter on Bows) with tails are all we need to finish off this basic bud vase arrangement. You could add touches of a Manzanita branch, stem of pearls, your favorite sprig of filler, or a stem of eucalyptus... add something to follow through with the look you have chosen... or your theme.

Centerpieces Made Easy

To arrange in a larger vase you will follow the same instructions. You will use 2 or 3 stems of your web flower or greens, and then add as many stems of flowers as you wish. If you want to have a garden look use more greenery and filler flower. If you like the solid flower look... use less greenery, and use Hydrangea or something similar to help hold your flowers in place. The most important thing you can do is practice. Get 2 or 3 bud vases varying from 1/2 inch to 2 inches, purchase some test flowers, and practice. There is a feel to designing and practicing will give you an idea of what you like. Our bud vase example design is very basic, simple, and good size to in which to practice. Have Fun!

Now let's think of the décor around the vase. Maybe floating candles, a mirror, flower side pieces, to name a few and certainly some of the most popular.

> Remember the adventure shopping? The picture shows our bud vase we used for our flowers, and the two larger vases we will be using for floating candles.
>
> These pictures show our votive holders we will use for the candles and a flower bloom side piece. The glass is all different in style, but will work great.
>
> The best part is our cost for all the vases and votives you see in the picture was only $6.91.

Tips!

If your vase is larger than the ½-inch opening as we chose in this example, adjust the number of "web-like" flowers you are using. Use 2 to 3 Hydrangea or greenery stems to create the web to hold your flowers.

You will use the same design instructions, repeating the steps for inserting the flowers until you have the desired look.
Practice, Practice, Practice is the best advice.
That way you will know exactly what size of vase you are comfortable with.

Designing the day before the wedding is much more stressful than months before the wedding. Know what your limits are, the time required to make your arrangement, how many tables you will have to prepare for and what your set-up crew is able to do.

All of these details are important for the day of the event. If it takes an hour to do the arrangement, and you have 15 tables... you are looking at 15 hours of effort. This typically is a commitment of time that is unrealistic for one or two people the day before your event. Start looking for dependable helpers!

With candles lit... everything in their place... how will it look... maybe... similar to ...

1 Vase	$1.00	Local thrift store
1 Stem of Hydrangea	$6.00	Local vendor
2 Stems of Gerbera	$6.00	Local vendor
½ Yard of Wired Ribbon	$1.50	Craft store
Total Cost	$14.50	
Professional Florist Cost	$24.50	**Bud Vase only**
Your Savings Each!	**$10.00**	

We have designed a bud vase in yellow and white Alstroemeria with a silver ribbon. The Alstroemeria and greenery are silk. We have used only a portion of a larger stem of the greenery, and we put some clear gems in the bottom of the vase for weight. These can be done weeks ahead of time.
The cost breakdown:

2 Stems Alstroemeria	$1.75	Craft store on sale
1 Sm Piece of Greenery	$0.75	Value store
Vase	$1.00	Value store
½ Yard Wired Ribbon	$1.00	Craft store
½ bag of Gems	$0.50	Value store
Total Cost	$5.00	Bud Vase Only
Add 3 Votives & Candles	$3.75	
Total New Costs	$8.75	Silk Bud Vase /Candles
Professional Florist Cost	$24.50	Silk Bud Vase/Candles
Your Savings Each!	**$15.75**	

Centerpieces Made Easy

Adding the décor and enhancements around your centerpiece is the fun part! You add can as much or as little as you wish. The size of your tables will determine how much and where you place the items of décor. You want to PRACTICE your look. You will have your place settings, goblets, water glasses, salt and pepper; maybe water pitchers, butter, etc.

Balance the table appearance and leave a comfortable space for everything planned. Arrange and rearrange until you get the balance you like. Use our table setting drawings (Appendix C) to figure out the spacing of your guest tables and everything that is going to be placed on it. Draw up your plan, write out step by step instructions, include a picture of your set up, and give it to who will be in charge of the set-up. This will help eliminate confusion, keep everyone organized and have exactly what you envisioned.

For larger bud vases, use 2-3 stems of web-like flowers or greenery to help hold the extra flowers needed for larger opening. Next consider the quantity and the diameter of the stems of flowers and greenery you want to arrange in the vase.

Practicing will give you the exact look, and the quantity of what will fit into the vase. In our bud vases with a 2 inch opening, gems in the bottom, a branch of curly willow, Calla Lilies or Gerberas, Bear Grass, a large green leaf, filler flower and/or ribbon are all choices and options for a larger bud vase… again… Practice will determine your comfort level and the look you will ultimately decide for your centerpieces… and the cost.

We have an example of a bud vase grouping that couldn't be simpler. We have three vases that cost dollar each, and three stems of Hydrangea. Fresh-cut a stem of Hydrangea for each vase, set the three vases in the center of your table and then… Enhance!

Floating Flowers... So Easy

Anyone can design this arrangement without a lot of effort!

... Even if you have never worked with flowers before!

It does take some shopping, preparation and planning! We found this beautiful dish in a thrift store for $3.99! Keep in mind, if this design is something you like then plan to look in many thrift shops and maybe multiple times. The hardest part of these designs is the shopping!

We found several bowl containers that would work beautifully on our first try, but plan several months ahead to look around to find exactly what you would like to use. Plan to use dishes or containers that look different or vary, but they would have a commonality. For example they would blend together if they all had silver trim, they are all frosted, they all look on the vintage side, or they all are clear glass. You will use the same flowers and color and that will tie the look all together. Give yourself plenty of time for your shopping.

A beautiful dish, bottled water, floating candle, and a flower bloom(s) is all you need to start this centerpiece. We have added a mirror, a votive candle, and a flower bloom in a votive holder. This arrangement is one that will not take a lot of time to do and with your picture and instructions; your helpers can follow through with what you envision.

Centerpieces Made Easy

*Let's add the finishing touches you have envisioned, mirrors,
Candles, flower side décor, napkin ring,
and you can have a very romantic look that glows...*

You will need one container for each table. Maybe each table will have a different vase giving each table its own personality. To pull the room together will be your consistency in the use of flowers and color. There are many containers like the clear glass pedestal seen here and are available in craft stores, online, and in the big box chain stores. Check out websites like Craig's List. Do your research, know what you like, then find the best price!

Our costs on this arrangement were:

Mirror	1 @ $3.50	$3.50	Home improvement store
Candles, Small Floating	6 @ $0.65	$3.90	Craft and décor store
Gerberas	4 @ $2.00	$8.00	Your source will vary based on quantity
Candle, Floating 3"	1 @ $2.50	$2.50	Local craft store
Dish Container	1 @ $3.99	$3.99	Thrift Store
Votive Holder	6 @ $0.50	$3.00	Thrift Store/Dollar Store
Candles, Votive	6 @ $0.50	$3.00	Local craft store
Total Costs		$27.89	
Professional Florist Costs		$54.50	Complete Set Up, Mirror as a Rental
Your Savings Each!		**$26.61**	

*Use more or less of what we have listed.
This stunning look we designed for $27.89! You can do it too!
Prior Planning Preparation & Practice equals Perfect!*

Floating Flowers... Making it Crystal Clear

Crystal gels are used in the bottom of these glass pedestal vases, with mini hot pink Gerbera's, a silk Orchid bloom, a small floating candle, surrounded by votives of candles and a Gerbera placed in a votive holder sitting in front of the arrangement. Now you could add a mirror, square dinner plates, and your colored napkin with special matching napkin décor. This is a design that is very simple, easy to do, and is cost effective.

We paid retail cost for the container but if you do some adventure shopping you could probably save $6.00 to $8.00 a container. The day we went shopping there were many containers with the same look without the pedestal for $1.99.

Maybe your vases will be different on each table, but use that to your advantage. Each table can have a slightly different look. Maybe have a lace runner on one table, and a satin runner on another table. The consistency of color will tie them all together. For example, all runners could be ivory but different types of material.

Using the same type flowers and colors in the designs will make it look like it all belongs in the same room. Different containers might also include different heights of centerpieces. Imagine all the candles glowing at different levels. Here is why practicing is important. It will allow you to see your set up before you walk into the reception room the day of your wedding.

Our breakdown of cost of this centerpiece is as follows:

Votive Holders	6 @ $0.50	$3.00	Thrift stores (votives are different styles)
Glass Pedestal	1 @ $10.00	$10.00	Thrift & craft stores, wedding supplies
Mirror	1 @ $3.50	$3.50	Home improvement store
Gerberas	3 @ $2.00	$6.00	Local source or can be found on line
Crystals	1 @ $0.50	$0.50	Garden store or local nursery
Candles	6 @ $0.75	$4.50	Estimate, cost on candles vary
Silk Orchid Bloom	1 @ $0.90	$0.90	Craft store, discount store
Your Costs		$28.40	
Professional Florist Cost		$50.00	The florist's time is a cost factor
Your Savings Each!		**$21.60**	**If you have time you will save money**

If you have 15 tables to prepare you would save $324.00 by doing your own centerpieces.

Test products such as candles by burning them to see how long they last and how well they burn before you purchase a large quantity. Order some extra for backup!

Tip!
Please Please… Read the instructions on the package on how to dispose
of the crystal gels. They can cause sever plumbing problems
if you put them down any drain pipe

This arrangement cost is estimated at $28.40. If you go adventure shopping you could save even more! We found we could save $6.00 to $8.00 if you wanted to have the vases a little different style on each table. On 15 tables you would reduce your centerpiece cost as low as $20.40, and save an additional $120.00!

This is in addition to what you will save by doing your centerpieces yourself! A total of $444.00!

Go Adventure Shopping and make it a "game" to see how much you can save!

You will be the WINNER!!!

Floating Candles... Vases, Votives & Blooms

This very simple idea can reflect anything or any theme you may want. Go to your local dollar store and buy enough vases to have three vases for each table. In our example, we paid an average of $3.00 for the three main tall vases.

Go Adventure Shopping in the thrift stores. We also picked up 6 votive holders (per table) for $0.50 each for $3.00.

We also purchased three 3-inch Floating Candles ($3.00 each) and six 1-inch votive candles (50 cents each) totaling $12.00.

So far that is $18.00 per table.

Test your candles! They need to last through your reception.

Your choices of gems, marbles, pebbles, crystal shapes, would provide interest in the bottom of the vases. Fill the vases with the bottled water up to about 3-inches below the rim of the vase. Set the candle on top of the water being careful to keep the wick dry.

The mirror is $3.50. Polished rock cost $3.00 (gems could cost less). Silk blooms cost 90 cents each. Adding vases and candles this centerpiece costs a total of $25.40.

Of course there are many ways to vary the centerpiece to lower your cost. Use 3 votives instead of 6, and without a mirror it will also look good! With these changes the cost is only $18.90. Now, using a coupon or finding items on sale can save even more.

Centerpieces Made Easy

Options could be using a 1 inch floating candle in the votive holders, crystal gel in the votive holder with a flower bloom, floating a flower bloom in votive holder, or a combination of the three would look great.

Set the votives around the vases. We chose to use all candles, placed some polished rock on the mirror with silk bloom accents in front of the vase. We have done this arrangement with fresh blooms on each side of the arrangement at the base of the vases adding the color of the wedding. We also used two levels of water in the vases to allow the candles to glow at two levels.

Everything can be done with a drawn diagram, simple instructions and/or a picture given to a dependable helper. Light the candles about fifteen minutes before guests arrive. Very simple!

In our variations of this centerpiece, notice the different shapes of vases, varying levels of candlelight votive holders, and in our last picture of just the romantic candle light. The 8 inch diameter cylinder vase has polished rock, bottled water, floating candles in, out and around... so very simple! Use any shape and size of glass bowl or container, polished rock or gems, bottled and candles of your choice votive, floating or tea lights.

At the end of this chapter is a variation of this centerpiece that compliments the one you just viewed. Have two different styles of centerpieces on you tables... be creative!

Our breakdown of a typical floating 3-cylinder vase centerpiece cost is as follows:

Item	Quantity	Cost	Source
Vases – vary heights	3 @ $1.00	$3.00	Thrift store, discount or craft store
Votive Holders for Candles	6 @ $0.50	$3.00	Discount store, craft store
Votive Candles (10 hour burn)	6 @ $0.50	$3.00	Local craft store
3" Floating Candles (10 hr burn)	3 @ $2.50	$7.50	Local craft store
Polished Rocks (by the bag)	1 @ $2.50	$2.50	Thrift store, discount or craft store
Beveled Mirror	1 @ $3.50	$3.50	Craft store, home improvement
Silk Blooms	3 @ $0.90	$2.70	Craft store, discount store
Bottled Water (1 gallon)	1 @ $1.00	$1.00	Grocery store, etc.
Your total Costs		$26.20	
Professional Florist Costs		$54.75	Comments
Your Savings Each!		**$28.55**	**You do the shopping; have a plan for the set up... saves you real money!**

With any of the items we have used, you need to do a little research. Costs do vary in different areas of the country. We have used the prices of retail stores that anyone can purchase from. This centerpiece does not have any fresh flowers and can be planned and organized weeks or months ahead of time. Set up the centerpiece in practice, take a picture the way you want it and your dependable helpers can reproduce it to perfection!

Now....you know you can do it!!!!

For a centerpiece that compliments the Floating Candle centerpieces, use a little imagination. On half of your tables use a taller glass with a silk or fresh flower stem.

In this centerpiece you can use silk or fresh flowers. There will be lots to see when your guests walk in and view varied heights of vases and candlelight on their tables. Half of your tables could be with something similar to this centerpiece shown and the other half with the 3 cylinder Floating Candles (centerpiece in this chapter).

When using silks, be sure to use a good quality silk. Keep your guests guessing, fresh or faux!

Vases of Flowers and Candles…

Simple to do and can be very romantic with the candle glow. Each table can have a personality of its own, whether it is a different flower, a variance in the size, height or shape of the vase.

Here we have 3 vases all the same height and size. We found them at a store, which sells them for $1.00 each. The votive holders resemble crackled glass were also $1.00 each.

The gems at the bottom of all three of the vases were a total of $2.00; the three votive candles were $1.50.

We paid $2.50 each for the 3 inch floating candles ordering them online. Therefore, our total without the flowers is $17.00. Now… the flowers are up to you.

The kind of flower, in or out of season, will make a difference in cost and your look.

In our example, the bride used a Dendrobium Orchid. Orchids are a premium flower so check into the cost before you make a final decision… Your choice!

Let's say you have a budget of $2.00 a stem for your flowers. We used one stem per vase. You have a candlelit centerpiece costing under $25.00.

For candles glowing at varied levels, pour your water at different heights in your vases, like in our picture.

Our bride gave to her guests a CD of the bride and groom's favorite songs with the cover in wedding colors. Nice touch for the guest when they are seated.

A great look with so many ways to enhance.

Vases	3 @ $1.00	$3.00
Votive Holders	3 @ $1.00	$3.00
Gems	1 @ $2.00	$2.00
Votive Candles	3 @ $0.50	$1.50
Floating Candles	3 @ $2.50	$7.50
Bottled Water	1 @ $1.00	$1.00
Flower Stem	3 @ $2.00	$6.00
Your Total Cost		$24.00
Professional Florist Cost Est.		$49.50
Your Savings Each!		**$25.50**

Multiply that times the number of tables you will have.
If you have 15 tables…

You have saved… $382.50!

Tall, Dramatic and Easy… Standing Tall

Two Tulips Standing Tall!

We have used clear gems, a submersible LED light and two white Tulips in a cylinder vase 18-inches tall with a 5-inch diameter opening.

Water is only a few inches deep, just enough to give the tulips plenty to drink. Tulips can be substituted with Roses, Calla Lilies or a favorite bloom that will be proportionate with the vase.

This centerpiece is great for the event with individuals who want to help you, that are dependable, but have never worked with flowers.

Preparation ahead of time is a must. Having as much as possible prepared ahead of time, will save you time before the wedding. It seems the last few days before a wedding or an event there is never enough time. Without enough time to do all those little details, will make a difference in the overall look of your event.

Prep ahead for this centerpiece would be:
1. Have all the vases and gems thoroughly cleaned.
2. Divide gems evenly, put in a little plastic bag, and place in the box with each vase.
3. Purchase your bottled water.

Day of the event:
1. Work on the centerpiece vases in one location of the room (rather than putting them on each of the tables). This will save time and a mess to clean up on the table linens.
2. If you decide to use an LED light, turn on the light, and add it into the gems. You may need to use kitchen tongs to avoid touching the side of the vase. Make sure the LED light is covered by the gems.
3. Add a few inches of water. Use a long-neck funnel so the water doesn't splash on the upper inside of the vase, or cause the gems to move too much exposing the LED light.
4. Hold the flower next to the vase. As in the picture you want the stem long enough to sit on the gems and the bloom with a few niches of the top of the vase. Fresh cut the stem of the flower on the end removing the extra length.

5. Hold the bloom of the flower gently, lowering the stem first into the vase. Place the flower in the vase of water adjusting if necessary to create eye appeal. Repeat with the second tulip at a different level than the first tulip.
6. Set the centerpiece on the tables! Pick the glass up with care ***always* supporting the vase from the bottom** and don't splash while walking! Once the vase is on the table, carefully place or slide the centerpiece to the center of the table.
7. Add your enhancements around your centerpiece. This centerpiece is wonderful for the warmer temperatures.

Our tulip vase has a romantic look, requires no floral experience, and is very budget friendly.

Vase or one similar	$8.00	Available online and in craft stores
2 Stems of Tulips	$5.00	Local vendor
Gems	$1.00	Local dollar store
Bottled Water	$0.25	Any grocery store
Submersible LED Light	$2.25	Craft store
Your Total Cost	$16.50	
Professional Florist Cost	$35.50	
Your Savings Each!	**$19.00**	Costs vary with flowers in or out of season; glass cost varies with vendors and the size of vase you chose. Shop around and use reliable vendors.

Now comes the fun part... add your décor of candles (if cooler temperatures), petals, bride and groom framed pictures, floating flower blooms, guest favors at their place setting, or bring out your theme all in your wedding colors....or...this centerpiece can stand alone quite beautifully! See our chapter on *Enhancements and... So Many Choices* for more ideas.

Choosing someone who is detailed oriented and reliable to set up the reception will make all the difference in your pictures, your stress level... and for your event to appear flawless!

Tall, Dramatic and Easy... Designed with Flair

*Tall, Dramatic and Easy... U*se the same instructions for this variation as the previous design.

This design stands tall in a trumpet vase complimented by sparkling clear glass gems with a submersible LED light providing a cool glow. Do you want more hint of color? Use some colored submersible LED lights in the gems, or use colored gems with the white LED light. Either way you add your color and an interest to your guest's tables.

The trumpet vase enhanced with three 3-inch glass cube vases floated the bride's favorite flower and glowed with the colored submersible LED lights amidst the clear glass gems.

Beautiful, Easy, Elegant...

The step by step instructions with pictures will make this arrangement very easy to do for anyone involved and wanting to help.

Chose a tall glass vase the size and shape you want. Our V-shaped vase is called a trumpet vase, 24 inches tall and 5 inches in diameter at the top and widest part of the vase. Thoroughly clean all vases. This vase narrows at the bottom and may require a cleaning cloth on the end of a thin cleaning brush or cloth covered stick to reach the bottom. Plan to clean ahead of time to save time before the event. Re-box your vases in their original shipping boxes to keep clean.

Decide if you will use colored or clear glass gems, colored or clear submersible LED lights. Chose the flower you want in your vase. Keep in mind the diameter of your vase. You do not want the flower looking smashed in your vase. We chose Dendrobium Orchids... they work perfectly with their size of he bloom and length of their stem.

Another decision we made was to fill the vase three-fourths full of water. This would the last step in the design, but you would need to plan to purchase the bottled water ahead of time. Bottled water guarantees a clear look in the vases.

Step 1.. Turn your LED light on and use your glass gems in the bottom of the vase covering the submersible LED light.

Turn on the LED light and place in the gems. We used tongs to avoid touching the glass vase

Step 2.. Pour a few inches of bottled water in the vase, covering the gems. A funnel will help you to direct the water, not splash, and prevent the gems from exposing the LED light.
Step 3.. Lower the Dendrobium Orchid stems first into the water and insert the stem in the gems.
Step 4.. With the funnel, pour water to the desired level carefully not to bruise the orchid blooms.

Step 5.. Before you finish filling the vase with water, take them to the reception area and set them on or near your table. Fill the vase with water to the level you want with the funnel. Carefully place or slide the vase by the base to the center of the table.

Centerpieces Made Easy

We used three 3-inch cube vases, the glass gems, and a submersible colored LED light, with a floating open bloom rose around this centerpiece. Allow time for the flower to open prior to the event.

We have the vases filled with bottle water to the level we want and placed the vase in the center of the guest's tables, the floating rose blooms are in their little cube vases and set around the trumpet vases. The bride added her special touches and we are ready for the guests to arrive. Additional vases were made for around the room, the cake table, displayed with the bridal bouquet, and the beverage table.

Many options are available for you with the Tall, Dramatic and Easy centerpieces.
Try different size vases and types of flowers. There is bound to be one you will really like. Then experiment with the flower of your choice. You want to be sure that the flower will hold up underwater if that is what you choose. Flowers can get slimy if under water too long. You can also use your favorite flower as we did with the tulips; just use a couple of inches of water. Experiment and practice!

This vase is 28-inches tall and 8-inches in diameter. We used two Gladiolas and a Rose in this bride's centerpiece. The advantage of the Gladiola, when in full bloom, is that it fills the vase with lots of color and they don't look skimpy. There are many flowers to choose from that would be great in this centerpiece. We have found that the most popular flowers are Orchids, Roses, Tulips and Calla Lilies for this vase arrangement. It looks great with or without the water filling the vase.

The vase alone in this picture was $28.00 retail. You can get a vase that is smaller in diameter which would be typically much less in cost. We have found them online for all price ranges... do your research for the best price. Once you know the look you want and size of vase, start looking for coupons to the craft stores, internet sites and in second-hand stores. The size of the vase will also help determine the kind of flowers to use and how many needed.

We added gems in the bottom of the vase to help hold the stems of flowers and to finish the look. Not filling the vase with water also makes it a little easier to work with. Flowers can be buoyant (or float) so practice, and know what you will face when you go to create your centerpieces for you big day!

	Low		High
Vase – 28 inches Tall & 8 inches Diameter	$10.00	-	$28.00
Gladiolas or Rose	$10.00	-	$15.00
Gems	$3.00	-	$10.00
Water	$1.50	-	$1.50
Your Total Cost Range	$24.50	-	$54.50
Professional Florist Cost	$65.00	-	$95.50
Your Savings Range Each	**$40.50**	**-**	**$41.00**

Your total for this centerpiece ranges from $24.50 to $54.50 depending on the cost of glass, and the flowers you choose. You can save approximately $40.00 per table with research, shopping and by you doing it yourself. Do not forget those coupons the craft stores love you to use!

Warning!
The thickness of glass varies and can break under the pressure of the water.
Be very careful handling the vases by always supporting the glass at the bottom.
Never grab vases by the rim to move them. The glass may break off in your hand!
Wear gloves when handling glass, prevents fingerprints and smudges.

This bride added touches that were special to her. As you see in the pictures, she started with basic arrangement, and then she chose to fill with water. She added all the touches that made it uniquely her….Origami's in her wedding colors.

Use a long neck funnel to fill your vases. It is not only easier and safer to reach the vase; the use of the funnel can direct the water with much more control and avoids splashing inside the vase.

Tip!
Tap water can be cloudy and diminish the look of your arrangement, so for absolutely clear water
Remember to always use bottled water!

When choosing the flowers, allow enough time for the flower to fully open. Gladiolas can take 4-6 days to fully open. Make sure to ask your flower vendor about your choice of flower and the length of time for the bloom to fully open. Calculate the number of days into your time table. For example: If the flower needs 4 days to open and a day to design the centerpiece. Possibly, you would need the flowers to arrive 5 days before the event.

This centerpiece is one prepared in the last few hours before the event and can be mostly done on-site.

Vases of all heights and diameter are available just about anywhere. So, with planning ahead, doing some shopping and armed with a couple of coupons, you can save more money and stretch the budget.

Determine if you want to fill your vase with water, and if gems, rocks or crystals would add interest for your centerpiece.

All these questions will be answered when you practice the arrangement well before the wedding date.

Tip!
Always wear gloves when handling glass.
It's safer and doesn't leave finger prints!

Warning!
If you are planning to fill the vase with water, make sure the glass is not too thin. Glass under pressure from the water can break the vase if it would get hit or bumped!
Plan to pour most of the water on site.

Rings of Beauty... Simply Done

Linda Boyko Photographer

Floral Rings are a real favorite. With today's variety of candles, fruit both fresh and faux, the shapes and style of glass for showing off the candle gives you many options. Your glass for the candle in the center can be a hurricane, or a vase in the center to hold water for a floating candle. This ring of flowers really doesn't need anything else to be beautiful, it can do it all by itself.

You can choose from a wide variety of flowers in this centerpiece. Use it to your advantage. Seasonal flowers will help keep the cost within your budget. Using faux fruit and dried items like lotus pods fills in larger spaces and would reduce the number of fresh flowers needed. The green apple in the arrangement looks real… it's not!

First depending on the size of your table, decide what size of floral ring you want to use. You will then have an idea of what type and size of glass for the center of the floral ring. Choices for the center could be a floating candle, a small one is about a 1¾ inches in diameter and a large floating candle is about 3 inches in diameter. Pillar Candles have many different heights and diameters. The candle should be proportional to the opening of the floral ring.

The choice of your glass depends on the look you want to achieve. Once you have made your choice of candle, floating or pillar, it will help determine the type of glass you will need. We show pictures using a 3 inch floating candle in two sizes of glass vases and a pillar candle with a Hurricane Shade.

Linda Boyko Photographer

Photography by Modern Grace Images, Shawna Clark

We used a vase 6 inches tall with an 8 inch diameter for this creamy colored floral ring and floated a 3 inch candle. Using a larger diameter glass vase, you could use two to three smaller floating candles as another option.

We used roses as our primary flower and Alstroemeria to fill in the gaps. You can follow the instructions of Rings of Beauty to design this centerpiece. This design can use just about any kind of flower and be stunning!

The tableware, the china, goblets, a creamy colored floral rose ring with the 6-inch cylinder vase floating a 3-inch candle are all in place...see it from your guest's point of view. An extra touch of elegance, the beautiful embroidered white overlay on her table.

With a great photographer, they will be able to take beautiful pictures of your centerpieces and show how the centerpieces created an ambiance for your guests at the reception.

In the picture we show a floral ring of pink flowers encircling the hurricane glass with a pillar candle. We show this hurricane shade as one type of glass that can be used with a pillar candle. The hurricane shade is protective only (it does not hold water). Most venues require protective glass with an open flame candle. It would be good to ask your coordinator what their policy is, if an open flame will be a part of your décor.

A vase sitting in the center of the ring can accommodate either a pillar candle or floating candles. With vases so readily available, and having varied price points, you might find the vase fitting the floral ring more cost effective than the hurricane shade.

In most stores you will have a choice of at least two sizes of floral rings. Once a decision has been made, choose the glass that will go in the center.

Tip!
It is important to carry your measuring tape!

Measure the bottom of the vase at its widest point and measure the widest point across the inside portion of the floral ring, is crucial to ensure they will fit together. It will save a lot of frustration when it comes time to putting your design together.

You may want to shop around first getting all the supply costs, and then figure out which size would work best for your budget. Keep in mind that the larger the space, the more product needed.

If you are using 8-top tables for your reception (tables seating 8 guests), you might find the smaller ring will work out great along with everything that would be added to the décor and function of the table (salt, pepper, water pitchers, etc.). Let's design!

With a decision of using a vase, you could make it an eclectic look. Go *Adventure Shopping* in the thrift stores… you could find a wide variety of vases at a fraction of the cost.

Go ahead and be adventurous!

Rings of Beauty... Done Well

We will provide step-by-step instructions for a beautiful centerpiece consisting of flowers, greenery and ribbons for more color. You can use any combination of flowers you like but the main thing is to practice to make sure you know exactly how it all comes together. You can then instruct your helpers of exactly what you envision your centerpieces to look like on the guest's tables. We can design this centerpiece with a mix of fresh and/or silk flowers. If you use all silk flowers using a Styrofoam ring, you can prepare your centerpieces way ahead of time.

This design can use as many or as little flowers as you wish. Depending on the look you prefer, you can a use a solid flower look using very little or no greenery. Or you could use greenery with a few choice flowers and maybe tucking in some ribbon for décor and color. Whether you choose to use fresh blooms or silk, we will show you how to get your design started, and you will determine the final look.

Practice with one floral foam ring by using the following basic instructions. If using **silk flowers** make sure you **use the Styrofoam ring**!

First, lay out the floral rings so that you can work on more than one centerpiece at one time (unless this is your practice run). Double check making sure that the vase you selected fits nicely in the center of the ring. Start by soaking the floral foam rings. Hold the ring with the foam facing down and gently lay it on top of the water. Let the foam ring soak at it's own pace. DO NOT push it under the water. Bubbles are good! You do not want any air pockets in the foam. Once soaked, lay the ring on your counter right side up.

Flower Placement is the next step in the design. If you like the flowers evenly placed, picture in your mind the centerpiece divided into three sections, like a pie. We have taken 3 floral wires and laid them

Centerpieces Made Easy

on the foam ring separating the ring in three even parts. Then lightly push the wire into the foam to create a slight line or indentation. This will help you evenly place the flowers.

In the center each of the three sections, you will insert your primary flower (your first choice or favorite flower, a Rose, Gerbera, Spider Mum, etc.). If you look close, you can see a line in the foam. We are inserting our first primary flower in between the marked lines, in one of the pie sections. The stem should be inserted an inch into the floral foam to make sure that the flower is firmly in place.

Insert another one of your primary flowers in each one of the three sections maintaining our three "pie" sections with a flower in each.

Next we are going to take our secondary flower (in our example, the Hydrangea) and fill in around the Gerbera. Hydrangea is wonderful for filling in space! For this design we will break apart the Hydrangea in smaller sprigs and insert next to the primary flowers you have chosen.

Insert the Hydrangea around each of the 3 flowers. Insert your next flower in between the 3 flowers you have already put into the floral ring. In our example it will be another Gerbera. You can use the same flower as in our example, or use a different flower, like a Rose, Mum, Daisy, etc. Then you will repeat the same steps as before.

Continue with the Hydrangea around the second set of primary flowers you have inserted. As you can see we still have floral foam showing that needs to be covered.

Tip!
Mixing in quality silk or latex premium flowers
can give the look you want and save you money!

Orchids are a premium flower no matter what the season. If you take some time and do some shopping, you can find some beautiful silk or latex Orchids that are incredibly real looking! We are sure you have seen them in many craft-type stores. Instead of $10.00 to $15.00 dollars for a fresh Orchid bloom... how about 90 cents! So let's mix some in our arrangement.

We chose a latex stem of Phalaenopsis Orchid. Cut each bloom from the stem using wire cutters and insert into the arrangement between other flowers.

You will still have some spaces that we will fill in with a ribbon loop. If you prefer not to have ribbon, fill in with some Hydrangea, filler flower, more silk blooms or whatever flower you wish. Be careful not to overwhelm the design. Filler flower is exactly that, it fills in. Filler flower should cover the bare spots of floral foam and not stick out too far for this design. A little sprig should work great.

A whole stem would be too large, so use a sprig, or small portion of the stem. A stem will go a long way to filling in gaps in the arrangement. We are going to use a little Eucalyptus Leaves for interest and accent. Cut a leaf where it connects to the main part of the stem. Insert a few leaves around the ring and fill in where the floral foam is showing.

Close-up of the flower ring shows the mixture of real and latex flowers.
Looks good but we're not done yet.

Adding a loop of wired ribbon can be added to represent a wedding color that may not come in flowers. Sadly not all the fashion colors can be represented by live flowers.

A ribbon accent can bring in a fashion color not available in flowers; fill a space where floral foam is showing. It is cost effective and looks beautiful! A perfect accent!

See our Chapter on *Making Perfect Bows Everytime* to make this ribbon loop.

Look for any bare spots where the floral foam is showing and fill in with a bow, filler flowers, or an extra bloom. Tuck in the ribbon where it might be needed to fill in a space and help cover the floral foam. Fluff the loop and arrange the tails of ribbon.

The estimated cost for this centerpiece is based on local shopping, *Adventure Shopping* and online shopping. Your resources and the time spent researching could prove to be even more cost effective.

Example Centerpiece			Variation		
Floral Foam Ring	1 @ $7.00	$7.00	Floral Ring	1 @ $7.00	$7.00
Mini Gerberas	6 @ $2.00	$12.00	Gerberas	3 @ $2.00	$6.00
Hydrangea	2 @ $5.00	$10.00	Alstroemeria*	4 @ $1.25	$5.00
Silk Blooms	6 @ $0.90	$5.40	Hydrangea	2 @ $5.00	$10.00
Eucalyptus Leaves	1 @ $2.00	$2.00	Greenery	1 @ $2.00	$2.00
Ribbon Loop	1 @ $1.50	$1.50	3 inch Floating Candle	1 @ $2.75	$2.75
Center Vase	1 @ $5.00	$5.00	Center Vase	1 @ $5.00	$5.00
1-3 inch Floating Candle	1 @ $2.75	$2.75			
Total Cost		$45.65			$37.75
Est. Professional Florist		$75.00			$69.00
Your Savings Each!		**$29.35**			**$31.25**

*Alstroemeria stems can have 3 to 5 or more blooms per stem. In addition, although most items can probably be purchased locally, but as you know everything is available online.

With your basic arrangement done, you might have ideas how you will do it differently for your wedding. You can change the flowers to a seasonal mix; make the entire centerpiece in silks, do your research.

Write down everything you intend to use for your arrangement: flowers, supplies, floral foam, ribbon, silk flower, etc. for a single centerpiece. Adjusting for any changes to the basic arrangement you wish. You now have a "recipe" for your design. Multiply by how many guest tables you will have. Make your shopping list and start price shopping! Watch for those valuable coupons for the craft stores and go adventure shopping for the glass. Most of all have FUN!

Choosing your glass container for the center of your arrangement could all be the same for each table or each table could have its own look.

We've also included some pictures of a glass container with a pedestal in the center. This gives some height and in this example we used crystal gels instead of water.

We placed the arrangements on a beveled mirror. We varied our look by using two types of candles in glass holders; some were floating candles and some were votive candles, making the perfect glow.

Do not give up the candle glow because it will be warmer or HOT for your event date…! LED lights are available in every size and shape; even the floating LED lights are an option for the warmer temperatures. They glow beautifully.

Photography by Modern Grace Images, Shawna Clark

This ring of flowers is the same one we just designed; only we have substituted different glass for the vase in the center. This glass container has a pedestal to give it some height. We used crystal gels instead of water, and placed a candle in the center. A floating candle in water works beautifully too!

It is time to test your centerpiece. Set the arrangement in the center of a dining table and sit down like you would as a guest at your wedding. Try to see what they would. See if there is any of the floral foam showing. If there is a broken flower or flowers inserted at an angle that may look odd, now is the time to fix it.

The face of the flower should mostly be facing out from the center of your arrangement. If there is some floral foam showing, fill-in with a sprig of greenery or some filler-flower. Keep in mind, every stem you use, adds up and you should take note if you are using more flowers in your practice run than you had planned.

Adding up each stem of the flowers used in your design will make up the "recipe", and then multiplying by the number of centerpieces you will need to make will be your flower order. Running short on flowers while trying to making your centerpieces would be a stress you would not want to face the day before your wedding. So order some extra flowers for breakage, wilting and unforeseen problems that may occur. Flowers are not all perfect, and having extra is always a good idea. We recommend at least 10% of your order as extra flowers. It is better to be safe than run out of flowers, especially if you have not done this before.

Completing your arrangement is the fun part! For the day of the wedding, with your vase in the center of your arrangement, fill your vase with the bottled water to the desired level using a funnel. Place your candle on top of the water or gels, keeping the wick dry, and then light your candles fifteen minutes before the guests arrive.

Tip!
Find out from your venue if their event planner will light the candles
at the appropriate time or should you have someone responsible for it.
Make sure you have at least two lighters
for your helpers to light candles!

Tip!
Also give your helpers the extra flowers to replace any flower breakage or to fill in.

Start with the Basics... Make it Your Own!

This centerpiece has versatility and elegance. If you look closely the arrangement in the silver vase and the arrangement sitting atop of the clear pedestal is the same arrangement! Make this centerpiece and create variations on each table... beautifully!

Step 1.. Select an inexpensive container with the sides of the container approximately 1-inch high and with a 6-inch diameter.

In our example, we chose a Mache container that is 6-inches in diameter and one inch deep. You could also use something plastic or a sturdy plant liner. This container is a throw away type container that will give you the versatility to place on top of another container or set in a vase. We will show examples of both options in this chapter.

Your finished arrangement in this container will also make it easier to transport (important!).

Step 2.. Next let the floral foam brick soak. Remember to not force the soaking by pushing down on the floral foam. It will soak quickly.

Step 3.. Measure and cut floral foam to fit snugly in your container.

Step 4.. Imagine your floral foam cut in fifths, like a pie. Each of the five primary flowers will be in one of these sections. You will choose your primary flower (ours is the Anemone) and after your fresh-cut, you will begin by inserting a single stem into each of the five "pie-sections" areas.

Step 5.. Give a fresh-cut and leave the stem about 6 to 7-inches long.

Hold the flower at the end of the stem where you have just done the fresh-cut, then guide and insert into the floral foam about an inch. You want to use this technique of stem insertion into the floral foam to prevent stem breakage (and cost more money).

Step 6.. Continue with the remaining four flower stems inserting in all the five pie-sections.

The perception should be that the flowers are radiating from the center of the design. This is an important visual appearance in flower arrangements.

Looking down on the design the blooms of the flowers would create a circle. This is your basic design shape.

Step 7.. Now for the height of the design, using your primary flower, fresh-cut the stem leaving about 7-inches in length and Insert the stem into the center of the floral foam about an inch.

If this is your first attempt at designing, follow the dimensions in the instructions. This will give the feel of the design.

Step 8.. For our secondary flower, we chose the Daisy Mum, but we need to separate the blooms. Pull off or cut the stem with the bloom from the main stem. Then carefully lay the blooms aside on a towel or soft surface to protect the petals.

Centerpieces Made Easy

Step 9.. Using your secondary flower (or continue to use all the same flowers if you like) insert it between the flowers you have already put in the floral foam.

Fresh-cut the secondary flower (the Daisy Mum) to same length, or as close as possible to your primary flower (the Anemone), position and insert into the floral foam in-between the bottom row of primary flowers. Try to avoid the flowers appearing in too much of a line.

Turn the arrangement a quarter turn in either direction to see the arrangement from a different angle, continue inserting your secondary flowers between the existing flowers. Simply turn the arrangement again and continue.

Tip!
Flowers are a part of nature, and nature does not always bloom perfectly. It is a matter of what you prefer, but sometimes having arrangements not "perfect" can even work out better!
They may have more of a
natural garden look.

While turning your arrangement, you can see where you need to adjust the design to keep it basically round. Try to limit your re-insertions because the floral foam is not meant to be reused or have excessive holes being made. The floral foam will fall apart if perforated too much… and you would have to start over.

Step 10.. Now we fill in spaces. In this example we will use our Cushion Mums. You will keep turning the arrangement, filling in the spaces, and keep the flowers spaced in between the flowers already inserted. As you insert the flowers, try to keep the basic round shape. You will have some open spaces between the flowers when you are done with this step. But you still have the greenery and filler flower too add to the centerpiece. So, let's start with the greenery.

Step 11.. We chose two greens, Geranium leaves and Maiden Fern (or your choice of greens). If you use Geranium leaves, the leaves can sometimes be turned inward or convex as in the picture. Hold the leaf with your fingers behind the leaf and your thumbs on the top of the leaf edge. Gently push with your fingers to turn the leaf out or concave in look (see the chapter on *Tips and Preparation* for additional choices of greenery for centerpieces).

Insert the leaves in-between the flowers. One word of advice is to not be too "heavy" on the greens otherwise you'll begin to lose the design. We still have to "fill- in" with filler flower. You will have a chance at the end to inspect if any you might need an extra bloom or leaf to cover the floral foam.

Step 12.. Fresh cut the Maiden Hair Fern in sections. You do not need use a full stem. We are cutting the fern above the last "branch" of the fern. Pull or cut apart the sprigs of greenery, you will use the fern so save all the sprigs. When you do the final inspection, you will find little spots in your arrangement that might need a little filling in and those little pieces of greenery will fit perfectly! Keep turning the arrangement to prevent a lopsided effect and to ensure the basic round design.

Step 13.. Use your next flower. We are adding Alstroemeria blooms. There are 4 to 5 blooms on a stem. Break the stem of the bloom off the main stem and use 2 to 3 blooms individually in your design. Give a small fresh-cut and insert in the spaces between flowers. Keep turning your design (using the container and not grabbing the flowers) and check that your basic round shape is consistent. If you need to shorten the length of a certain flower, simply pull the flower out, do a fresh-cut on the stem and replace in the floral foam.

Step 14.. Optional: Take an Alstroemeria stem with 2 to 3 blooms, do a fresh-cut on the stem leaving 6-7 inches. Insert into the floral foam towards the top of your arrangement.

Centerpieces Made Easy

Step 15.. Add touches of filler-flower to add interest and fill in the spaces between flowers. We used Wax Flower and Misty White. Remember to break up one stem into smaller stems leaving them long enough to fill in the spaces. Add the amount of filler flower to your liking.

Step 16.. Here is your chance to fill in any bare spots and make sure that the floral foam is covered, but not to over do it. You want to have a basically round centerpiece... not lop-sided.

> *FINISHED! Now for the final look.*
> Set up your arrangement on your table and sit as a guest. See if any foam is showing. In this design, flowers don't need to be perfectly spaced, but you do need to let the flowers have some breathing room and still keep the basic design round. Add or replace as needed.
>
> When preparing the design, invite your helpers and use a production line (see in the chapter Tips and Preparation) to make your centerpieces.

The costs break down for this arrangement is based on some flowers that are seasonal. Substitutions can be made to a flower of similar size. This arrangement has a great deal of flexibility. Pick your combination of flowers and do your costs break down to fit your budget. This arrangement can be placed in most any kind of container or set on a pedestal. We have shown several ways to set up this design. There are 3 sizes of arrangements and small enhancements of floral touches, all very easy to do. For the cost of this basic arrangement, its look is of a much greater value.

Mache Container	$0.75
5 Anemones (Seasonal $2.00ea, Mini Gerberas could be a substitute)	$10.00
2 Daisy Mum Stems ($1.50ea)	$3.00
1 Cushion Mum Stem	$1.50
1 Stem of Misty, Baby's Breath or Wax Flower	$3.00
Choice of Greenery, See our chapter *Tips and Preparation*	$3.00
Total Basic Cost	$21.25

You will still need to select the container to display this centerpiece.

Practicing will be very important. Practicing will let you know the quantity of flowers needed and what you like and don't like. After determining the amount of flowers needed for your arrangement you will multiply it by the number of tables you are planning to have at your event. This will translate into the number of bunches you will need. You will then have a good idea of the cost

NOW… let us see how the arrangement can be versatile.

The fun part is here! Enhance and add your favorite décor to complete the look of your table.

We have shown a clear glass vase turned upside-down as a pedestal for our arrangement.

Our arrangement is sitting on top of the bottom of the vase. This allows you to drape flowers, greenery, pearls, lace, ribbon, or whatever you can imagine.

We tucked some Hanging Amaranthus at the lip of the container to allow some texture and interest. We also added some Maiden Fern hiding our throw-away container.

We added enhancements of matching flower side pieces, they are in plastic silver containers with a beautiful glossy finish that has a look of a greater value, and would fit the budget well. Our vase is about 3½ inch diameter and 4½ inches tall.

Using some of your left over flowers, you can make this little accent arrangement. It is perfect for a companion piece for the guest's tables, cocktail tables, bar, cake table, guest book table and small guest tables.

We added a draping of Hanging Amaranthus for a dramatic effect, but you can use another vine type greenery.

Group together a small bouquet about 4-5 inches in diameter and use a pipe cleaner or wire to hold the stems together.

Make up all the little bouquets, give them a fresh cut and put in a small bucket of water with a couple of inches of water. Make sure all the flower stems are in the water.

On the day of the event, line up your vases, put water in the vase, then take out a little bouquet cut stems to fit, and place in the vase. Done!

Centerpieces Made Easy

Our companion arrangement is made exactly like the basic arrangement that we did in the first part of this chapter. It is designed in a silver plastic container about 6 inches in diameter. We used the Daisy Mums as the first and primary flower. This arrangement is smaller, uses less flowers than the first arrangement making it a perfect companion. This size would be good for tables that would seat four people. Proportion is important in everything we do. Having an arrangement too small or too large for the space can look odd or not well thought out.

In the following pictures we have set the original arrangement in a silver pedestal container that can be found in a variety of stores. What a difference in your look! By arranging the centerpiece in a throw away container, you can easily transport them sitting flat. It gives you flexibility in the look of the room allowing you to set up your centerpieces differently on the guest tables. For variety, try putting some of your arrangements on top of a turned upside-down pedestal vase, and other arrangements in a low container type vase. This will give your reception area varying heights of centerpieces making a beautiful visual when walking in.

In the centerpiece we have tucked in some Hanging Amaranthus and Maiden Hair Fern at the lip of the vase. You can substitute other greenery for draping or... nothing is required!

Step 17.. Enhance your centerpiece with groupings of candles in goblets, votives or vases. Make companion pieces in small vases, or votive holders with leftover flowers. Decorate the bar, cocktail tables, sign-in tables or restrooms with small accents of flowers. In these pictures we purchased the goblet for a $1.00 and the votive cup was 50 cents.

Varied heights of the arrangements and by adding some of the enhancements make it interesting to the eye.

We have added five mini Gerberas in a small clear glass vase (in front of the tallest arrangement), one Gerbera in a votive cup, and a floating candle in a goblet.

You can make one of these arrangements or all them. You could put one arrangement on a smaller table or use three for the larger tables... so many options with this very basic and beautiful design!

Flowers With Double Duty... Dual Use

Flowers can be used in two places quite easily.

We are showing two examples of flowers used in the ceremony, then moved to the reception.

This allows you to have the look of more flowers. You will be framed by beautiful flowers as you come down the aisle, then your guests will enjoy them on their table as they dine.

Aisle flowers are in the container hanging on Sheppard Hooks placed next to the chairs for the ceremony.

The arrangement is designed in a separate container that can be lifted out of the hanging container.

Once the ceremony is over, the arrangement is lifted out and taken to the guest tables.

The flowers are now the centerpiece for your guests to enjoy!

Plan ahead.

The person or persons to help make this happen need to be identified early. If you have a wedding planner, coordinate with them, or delegate!

These summery flowers are arranged in the galvanized pail used in the ceremony, and then taken to the guest tables to become the centerpiece.

If you have 10 aisle arrangements (5 on each side), and you are planning to have 15 guest tables, you have already taken care of two-thirds of your centerpieces. Plan ahead who will carry them to the guest tables.

It allows you to have a nicer centerpiece when you have a dual use arrangement…and pictures are gorgeous!

These arrangements require time and preparation. We advise that this be a job for someone with a creative eye and can spend three days being focused on the flowers.

You will prepare this arrangement as the basic arrangement in *Start With the Basics… Make it Your Own!*

It may be difficult to be involved in the wedding and try to do this arrangement… but it can be done!

You would need some good help, a plan, and… Practice!

Hydrangea… Effortless Elegance

This centerpiece requires so little time, no experience with fresh flowers, but looks like you have devoted so much to it. An arrangement that requires so little effort, versatility and elegance, could be the choice for you.

The flower shown is the Hydrangea. Your Hydrangeas should be fully hydrated and ready to use. See our Chapter on *Tips and Preparation* for more information on the care of your flowers.

Step 1.. Choose your clear or colored glass. The container should be approximately 6 inches deep to ensure the stems have room to be placed in the vase. Hydrangea needs more water than the average flower and would work best in a vase of water rather than the floral foam. We chose a vase 6 inches tall with a diameter at the top of 8 inches. Our curved sided vase is perfect for this arrangement which also provides support for the Hydrangea blooms.

Step 2.. Place clear gems in the bottom of the vase. Pour bottled water into the vase about three inches below the rim. An optional item we used was an LED submersible light in the gems.

Step 3.. Strip off all leaves from the stem of the Hydrangea.

Step 4.. Give the Hydrangea a fresh-cut leaving the stem approximately 5 inches long.

Step 5.. Place the stem in the vase with the stem going into the gems.

Step 6.. Repeat with the second and third stems of the Hydrangea.

Step 7.. Set up your dining room table as you would for your event. Add the enhancements you have planned. Set it up the way you want for your event. Take a picture and write out instructions for your helpers. Record your time, and list out everything that you have used in your arrangement. You will multiply by the number of tables you are planning at your event so that you can compile your supplies and flower order.

This is truly a do it yourself centerpiece that anyone can do and looks like you are the professional. In our centerpiece we also added an LED submersible light to add a glow in the vase. LED lights are an excellent way to provide a glow instead of candles in the warmer temperatures. Continue to add items around your vase that would compliment and carry through with what you envision.

Remember to take a picture, and write down your instructions in detail for your helpers. On the day of your event you will find there will be less stress and set up will go much smoother. If you are the bride your **only** job is to look beautiful for pictures!

Glass is readily available. We chose a vase a little more up-scale. You can use a wide variety of styles with this arrangement. Ceramic and colored glass is also an option to carry through with a wedding color. The cost on this centerpiece will vary with the glass and the flower vendor you choose

		Low	High	
1 Vase	1 @ $6.00	$6.00	8.00	Thrift store, dollar store
3 Hydrangea Stems	3 @ $6.00	$18.00	$18.00	Local vendor or online
1 Bag of Gems	1 @ $1.00	$1.00	$1.00	Dollar store
1 Submersible LED light	1 @ $2.25	$2.25	$2.25	Craft store
Your Total Costs Range		$27.25	$29.25	Do your cost research
Professional Florist Estimate		$42.00	$51.00	
Your Savings Range		**$14.75**	**$21.75**	It all varies on the vendor

This arrangement done with silk Hydrangea is an option, allowing you to have the centerpieces done well before the wedding date. Beautiful, full and could not be easier to do. Add all your enhancements to carry through with your theme or style.

Small and Simple… A Perfect Touch

Small and simple is the perfect touch for a cocktail table, bar accent, cake table, or have several along the edge of the head table between the girl's bouquets for quick and easy décor.

These floral touches are simply three flowers and little filler in frosted or clear vase (that come in a variety shapes). Choose any small vase whether square, oval, round or even a triangle. You can add the decorative touch to any area in the reception room. We added a lime or orange slice for added interest. You can get the orange or lime slice in plastic or use a fresh slice on the rim of the vase.

These may be small, but they can offer a spot of color on a cocktail table or the bar, any small area in where there may be a lot of activity.

These arrangements can be done with the flowers that you have left over from the centerpieces. Each one can have a personality of their own. They do not need to be exactly the same.

In your *Adventure Shopping* pick up a few small vases, have them clean and ready for last minute arrangements for that spot of color anywhere. Simple and easy!

Choose your vase and fill at least half-way with water. We chose a square vase about 3 inches across and deep. This little vase will hold more flowers than you might think.

These small arrangements are great for using the left over flowers. They are small enough for the little extra places you want to add color, maybe in a high traffic area like the bar, or a small area like a cake table, narrow shelf, bookcase, cocktail table, photo booth, just to name a few popular areas.

If the event is at night, add a submersible LED light in the water to give a little glow!

Instructions for *Small and Simple... A Perfect Touch.*

> **Step 1..** Hold the stems of flowers to be used in a small bunch like a little bouquet. Experiment with the size of bouquet to see the amount of flowers that will fit your vase best. The flowers should have a slight rounded shape with the center flowers slightly higher. If you need to tie the stems together use a pipe cleaner or a wire it will help hold the stems in place while you give the stems a fresh-cut.
>
> **Step 2..** Decide how long stems should be by holding the grouping of flowers up to the vase.
>
> **Step 3..** Give stems a fresh-cut the desired length using floral scissors or a floral knife.
>
> **Step 4..** Place the flower stems in the vase.
>
> **Step 5..** Decide if an extra flower or some filler flower needs to be added.
>
> **Step 6..** Add a bow, slice of fruit or something creative to add to the theme of the wedding.

Head Table

Planning to use your flowers and arrangements in **both** in the ceremony and at the reception, will stretch the budget! We designed a ceremonial arch topper that could also be used as the head table centerpiece. Showy, and smart! **Ask your florist if they can design your arch topper for a dual use**. Now, plan ahead...

The arch topper doesn't move itself.... After the ceremony and **after** your pictures are done, have a reliable person take down the arch topper and place it on the head table. We also have pictures showing a bride using her bouquet on the head table with floating candles in vases on each side. Another picture shows the head table with vases ready for the bridesmaid's to drop in their bouquets, combined with some additional flowers on the ends of the head table (from our chapter, Small and Simple) you have a beautiful head table from one end to the other. If you want to display bouquets, add the vases to your set up plan to ensure the vases will be there when you need them.

With these head table examples, there was thought given and a plan made. Moving the arch topper, and who was going to do it, is an important detail. Don't assume the venue coordinator will move it, ASK if they will help, if not, get a helper. Give some thought how you can use your flowers from the ceremony, in your reception.

The Pomander Kissing Balls can be moved to go around the cake, on each side of the gift table, or highlight the head table. Plan Ahead.

The decorated vases in the wedding colors were all part of the centerpiece planning and set up. We painted the ceramic vases the wedding color with a **non-flammable paint.**

The colors of this wedding were purple and sage green. The courtyard doubled as the ceremony site before the reception. An antique candelabrum used as a unity candle in the ceremony belonging to the bride's grandmother, then used on the head table as a centerpiece. We used oranges and limes in the guest's centerpieces providing beautiful color blending with the courtyard's natural beauty.

This Sweetheart table in purple, burgundy and cream, has a vintage look. The bride carried it through to her special place at the table. In the bride's Adventure Shopping she purchased a hat box, tea cups, a crumb tray, and added some framed engagement pictures of the bride and groom in an old fashion setting. Her table linen was a deep purple satin with a rose design. Her custom bouquet of feathers and wooden roses was a focal point of her décor.

Ask your florist to design your arch topper so that you can take out part or the entire arch topper and use it for your head table.

Centerpieces Made Easy

Napkin Décor

A little touch of interest on a guest's napkin can add so much. In this chapter we will show examples of some napkin décor that is easy to create, adds color, interest and texture. It also can be a little something for your guests to take home!

Draping this sweetheart table is beautiful black satin linen with a rose pattern. The bride chose matching black napkins. It needed a touch of the second wedding color… hot pink. We cut the stem off a Daisy bloom and placed it flat on the napkin. Using a flower like a mum or Daisy with several blooms on a stem will stretch the budget and add flair! Any helper can help with this idea!

This bride's favorite flower, the Gerbera, accented her guest's napkin and plate. Cut the stem of the Gerbera and place on the napkin. Hydrangea works beautifully also! …Quick and easy!

The butterfly napkin décor or the hot pink ribbon with pearl loop napkin decor (both pictured above) is created in the same way.

Step 1.. Our base for the butterfly napkin décor is a gold mesh ribbon 2 1/2 inches wide and cut 6 to 8 inches long. We made a bow of two loops of ribbon with tails (See our chapter on *Making Perfect Bows Everytime*). We hot glued the ribbon bow on the base ribbon.

Step 2.. There was an outdoor theme for this event, so keeping with the theme, we hot glued a butterfly and silk bloom in the bow… or in the elegant pink and black color scheme, we glued in a pearl loop and silk bloom in our bow adding a touch of elegance.

Step 3.. How to display your décor on the napkin is as easy as laying the décor on the napkin. Or you could glue a thin ribbon, decorative wire or twine on the back of the ribbon base allowing you to tie the décor around the napkin.

For napkin rings, we started with a ribbon circle or "ring "using a width of ribbon one inch wide. This "ring" is what the napkin will slip through, just like any napkin ring you might use. The diameter of the ring is important, and is relative to the thickness of your napkin you will be using. If possible, you want to test making a "ring" with the napkin you have chosen for your event, before you make 100 rings (or whatever your guest count is). If it is not possible to test ahead of time, increase the diameter of the ring to 2 inches to be safe. It would be better for the ring to be a little larger for the napkin to slip through with ease, than too small and cause a frustration the day of the event.

- **Step 1..** In making the "ring" part of the napkin ring, keep the diameter opening of the ring consistent. Find an object like a wood dowel, or piece of PVC pipe from a home improvement store that has a 1 ½ to 2 inch diameter (or what you have determined to fit the napkin)and about 4 feet long. Having this length will allow you to make several rings at one time, (since we used some PVC pipe, we will refer to the PVC in our instructions). Wrap your ribbon around the diameter of the PVC pipe. When cutting the ribbon, add an extra inch of ribbon allowing the ribbon to overlap itself. Glue or hot glue the ribbon between the overlapped ribbon ends. If you want to place a little piece of tin foil under the area where it will be glued, this will help with sliding the "ring" off the PVC pipe at the appropriate time. Continue to make the rings on the length of the PVC pipe leaving a little space between the rings. This allows room to work on them.

- **Step 2..** Make a bow out of some matching ribbon, twine, Raffia, cord, lace or something you would like to enhance the wedding colors or theme. After making the "bow", hot glue the bow on to one of the "rings" (we used the hot glue because of the quick drying time, but it can hurt if it drips on you!). Continue to make the bows and adhere to the rings.

- **Step 3..** What next? You decide! A touch of your theme, elegance or hobby will all work wonderfully. In our examples we have used silk blooms, dried leaves, peacock feathers, gold leaves, a ribbon cord, rhinestones, pearls, faux berries, twine and moss. Some other things we have used that are not shown are faux lime, orange or lemon slices, mini cars, boats (hobbies of the groom), Bling of all kinds, thank you's for the guest with a picture of the bride and groom tied or glued in.

However you decide to decorate your napkin, it is a fun project that can be done months ahead of time. If you decide to use ribbon, use wired ribbon. Wired ribbon can be fluffed up when it is time for use. You will avoid the ribbon being permanently flattened and have smashed loops! The examples we show are using décor that is "storable". We have used things that are silk or preserved and won't deteriorate. We stored them in a labeled tote box, and it's now ready to transport to your venue.

Appendix A… Centerpiece Cost Worksheet

Item Description	Number of Centerpieces	Number of Pieces per Centerpiece	Total Pieces Needed	Cost per Piece	Total Cost
	X	=		X	=
☐					
☐					
☐					
☐					
☐					
☐					
☐					
☐					
☐					
☐					
			Total Cost for the Centerpieces		
Enter Total Cost for the Pieces Here Too		Divided by Number of Centerpieces		Equals Each	

Estimate of Time Required to Construct Centerpieces

Number of Minutes to Make One	Number of Centerpieces	Total Minutes Required	Total Minutes Required Divided by 60	Round Up to the Nearest Hour
X	=		/ 60	=

Note: Don't forget you will need time to pack your centerpieces in boxes to transport them safely. Then you will have to carry them into your reception room and set them up. These are all time values that need to be factored in whether on site or at home.

This is the time you need to plan to make your centerpieces.

Appendix B... Tools and Supplies

List of supplies in the book... you may or may not need all of them depending on your desires.

Centerpieces Made Easy

Appendix C... Table Diagrams

Table Layout for 2-4 People, 36 inch Diameter

Table Layout for 4-6 People, 48 inch Diameter

Table Layout for 6 People, 60 inch Diameter

Table Layout for 8 People, 60 inch Diameter

Table Layout for 10 People, 72 inch Diameter

Table Layout for 8 People, 8 ft by 30 inch Rectangular

Reception Table for 2-4 People
36" Diameter Table

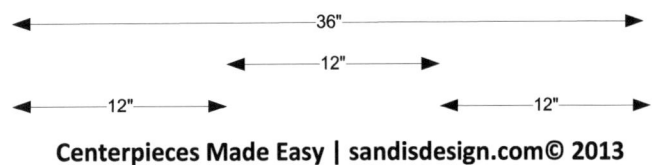

Centerpieces Made Easy | sandisdesign.com© 2013

Reception Table for 4-6 People
48" Diameter Table

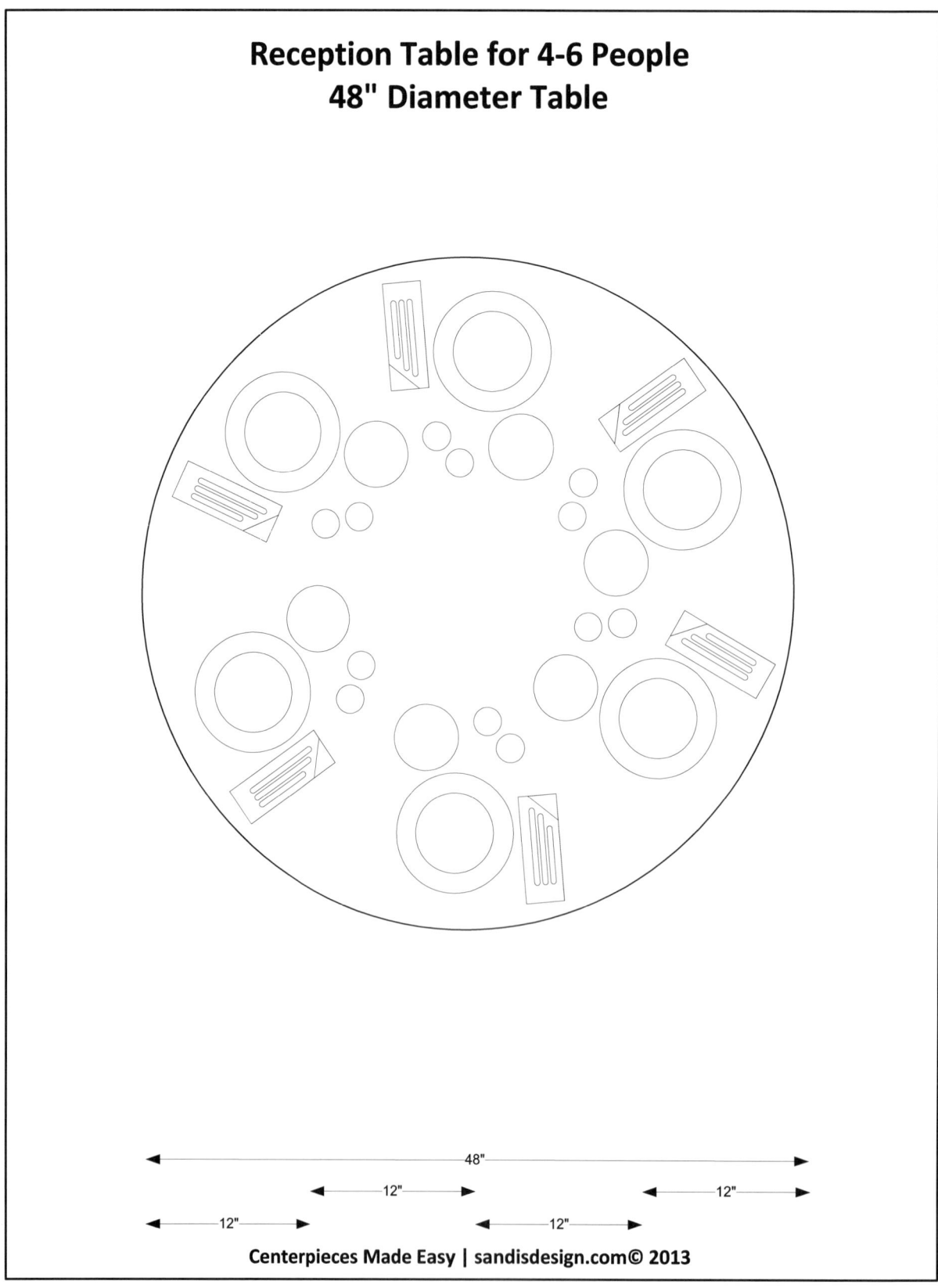

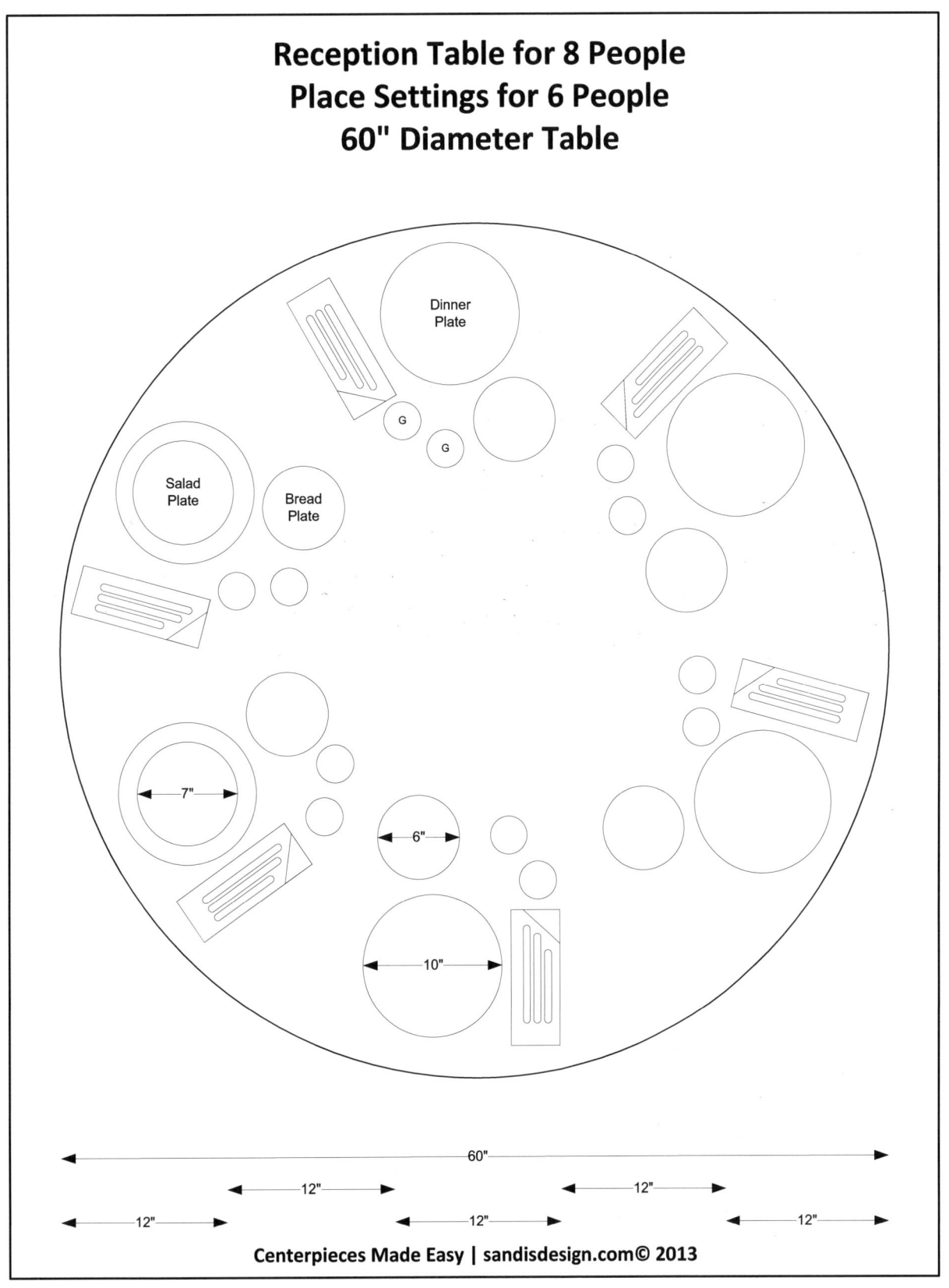

Reception Table for 8 People
60" Diameter Table

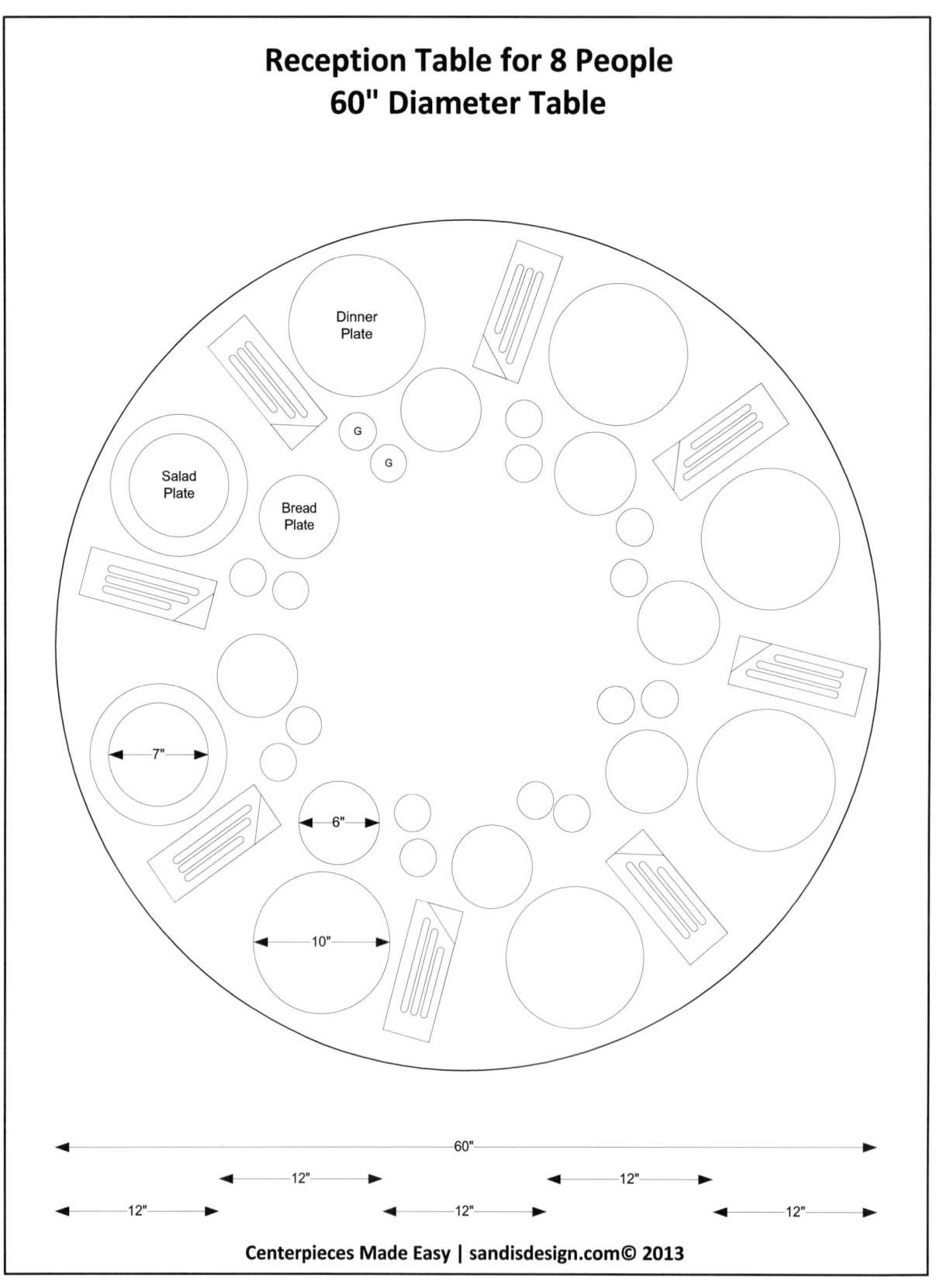

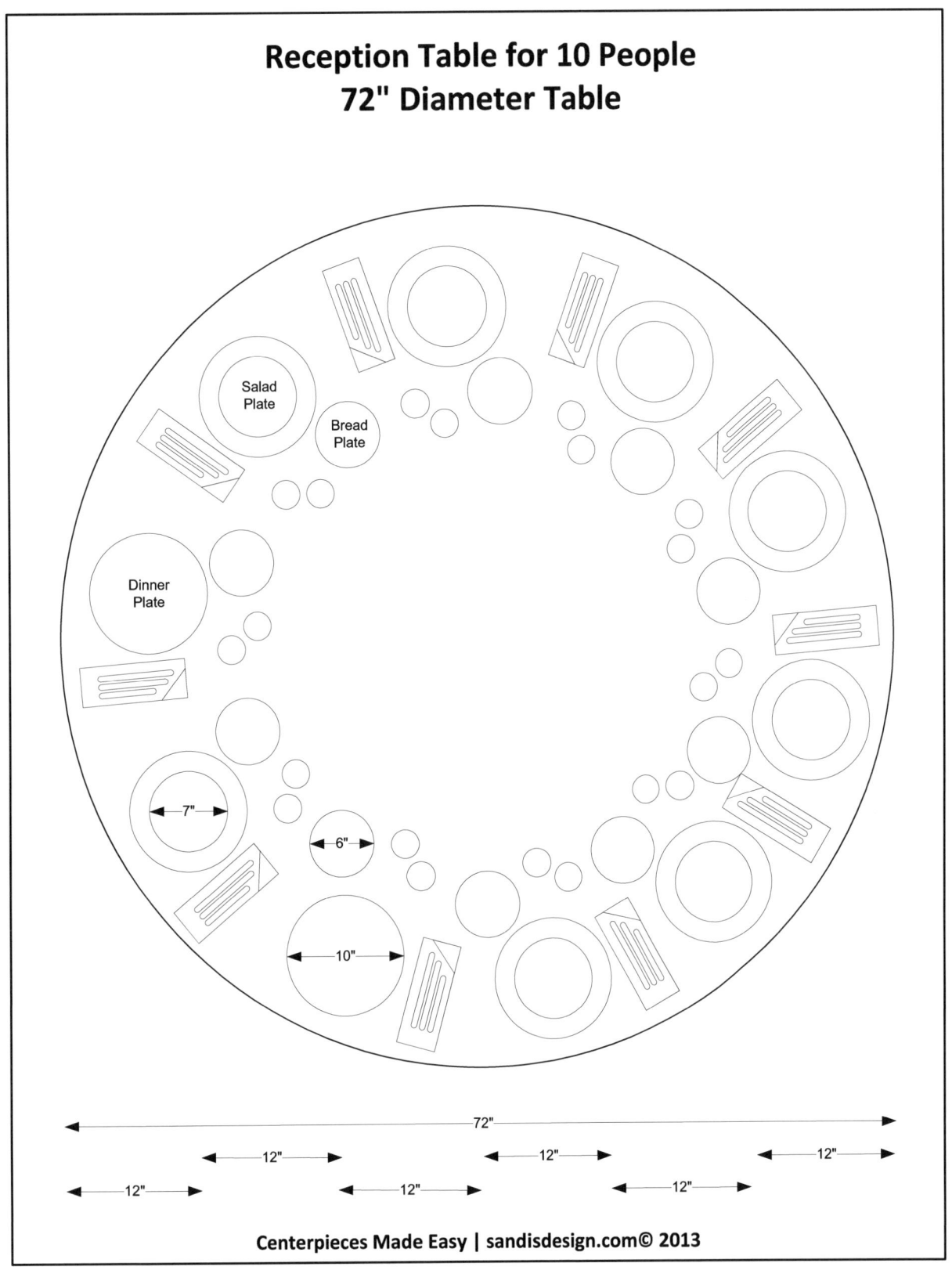

Reception Table for 8 People
8 ft x 30 inch Rectangular Table

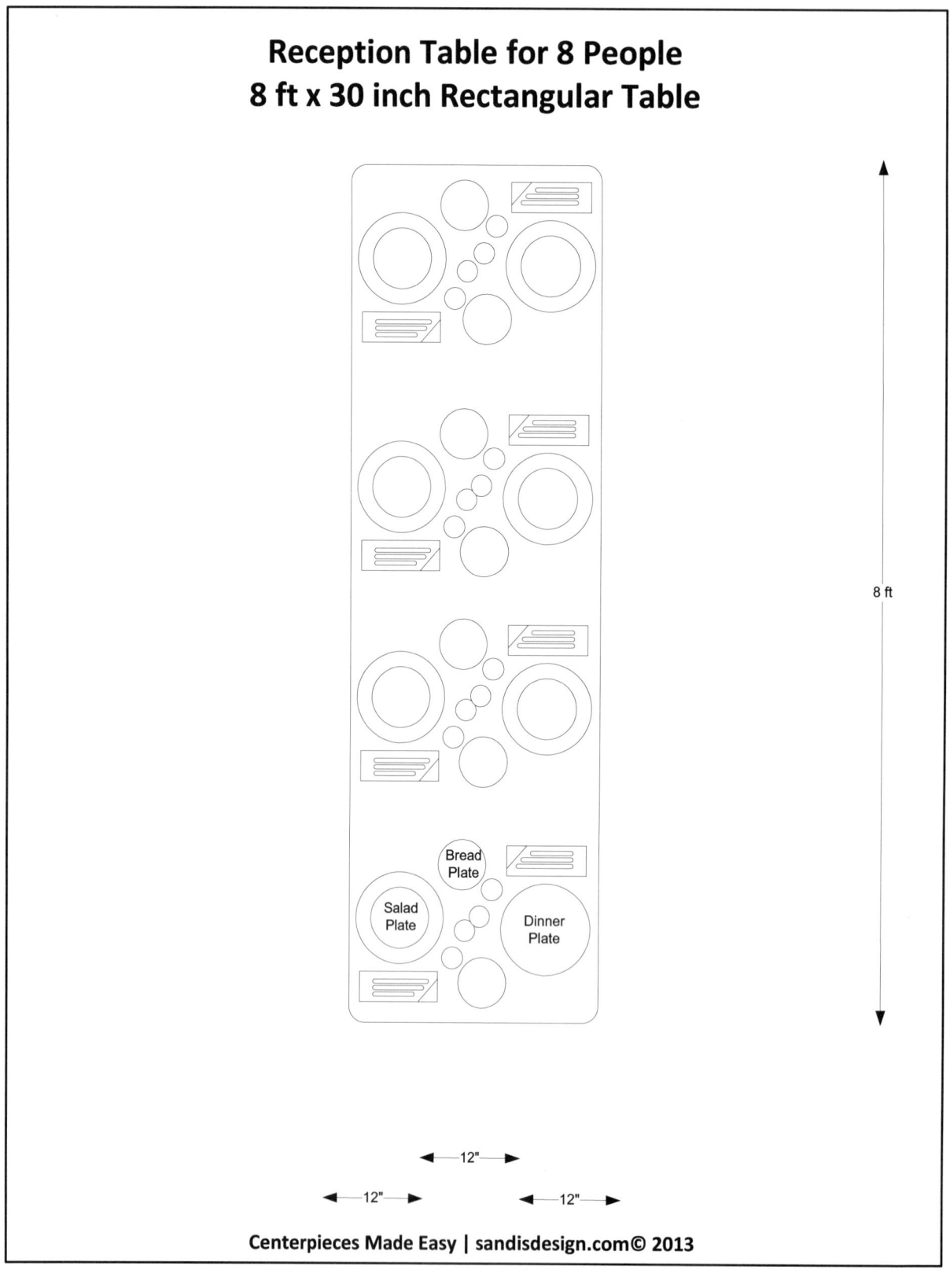

Centerpieces Made Easy | sandisdesign.com© 2013

Appendix D... List of Suppliers

This list of suppliers is by no means exhaustive but a start. By knowing the stores in your area, useful sources such as Yelp, or simple internet searching, you WILL find what you want. Remember *Adventure Shopping* in thrift stores, expanding to garage sales or flea markets for that eclectic touch. Except for perishable items, purchase your supply items well in advance of your event date. This allows plenty of time for any mistakes in ordering or breakage. Read reviews and recommendations. Test the vendor's products to ensure the product is the right color, the right size or amount and that it will work for you.

Supplier	Website	Products
Beverly's	www.beverlys.com	Vases, gems, filler, crafts
Big Lots	www.biglots.com	Vases, crafts, tools, etc.
Costco	www.costco.com	Fresh flowers and vases
Dollar General	www.dollargeneral.com	Crafts, tools, etc.
Dollar Tree	www.dollartree.com	Vases, gems, filler items
Family Dollar	www.familydollar.com	Vases and filler items
Flora Fresh	www.florafreshinc.com	Fresh flowers
Floral Supply	www.floralsupply.com	Floral supplies
Floral Supply Syndicate	www.fss.com	Floral supplies
Global Rose	globalrose.com	Fresh flowers
Goodwill	www.goodwill.org	Visit the stores
Green Leaf Wholesale	www.greenleafwholesale.com	Fresh Flowers, Supplies
Hobby Lobby	www.hobbylobby.com	Crafts, silk flowers, tools, etc.
Home Depot	www.homedepot.com	Mirrors and nursery items
Jo-Ann's	www.joann.com	Crafts, silk flowers, tools, etc.
Lowes Home Improvement	www.lowes.com	Mirrors and nursery items
Main Wholesale Florist	www.mainwholesaleflorist.com	Fresh Flowers, Supplies
Michaels	www.michaels.com	Crafts, silk flowers, tools, etc.
Modern Vase and Gift	www.modernvaseandgift.com	Vases, Supplies
Orchard Supply Hardware	www.osh.com	Gels, plants and nursery
Sam's Club	www.samsclub.com	Fresh flowers and vases
Save On Crafts	www.save-on-crafts.com	Crafts, tools, etc.
Walmart	www.walmart.com	Floral Supplies, Vases, Decor
Wholesale Flowers & Supplies	www.wholesaleflowersandsupplies.com	Fresh flowers, Supplies

Tip!
Test quality... Before buying quantity

ABOUT THE AUTHOR

Sandi Allcut has loved flowers and has been in the floral industry for over 30 years. Her interest in floral design began when her best friend did not have the money for her wedding flowers. Being creative, she designed fresh flowers for the first time. This began a life time of curiosity of learning floral design with emphasis on wedding flowers. Having been formally trained in floral design, interior design, and owning her own successful floral shop , she is an expert in floral design and believes that we are given one opportunity to deliver the wedding flowers that exceed expectations.

Sandi and husband, Gregg, currently own a custom floral business specializing in weddings and the special event. Combined with a God-given creative talent, the desire to create what the bride envisions, and a husband who has the project manger background, Sandi and Gregg, has developed a business model to give the highest level of personal service that a florist can give.
The brides selecting Sandi and Gregg as their floral provider have said...
They are more than just a florist!

"We had a great time writing a book that we hope will help start a plan, spark creativity, and help stay within a budget. Every bride deserves a centerpiece she will love at her wedding."

We wish you all the very best in designing,

Sandi & Gregg